The Place *Light* Gets In

BEVERLY BAKER • TONY CLARKE • STEFAN FATZINGER
CAROLYN FORE • CHRISTY BAKER KNIGHT
JEANNIE LONGLEY • SALLY PARSONSON • JANET WILSON

THE PLACE LIGHT GETS IN

Published by Holy Innocents' Episcopal Church

Book Production: Carolyn White Fore, Ph.D.

Editorial: Carolyn White Fore, Ph.D. and Sally Parsonson, Ph.D.

Cover and Interior Design: Peter Hildebrandt

Artistic Design: Christy Baker Knight

ISBN 978-0-578-33670-1

This book of memoirs is dedicated to Holy Innocents' Episcopal Church in Sandy Springs, Georgia, in appreciation for the support in spirit and resources provided to the members of our memoir group. All proceeds from sales of the book will be donated to Holy Innocents'.

Contents

About the Authors   261

About the Book   281

PREFACE

The memoir group which has produced *The Place Light Gets In* began in the fall of 2013 when the Reverend Martha Sterne and the Reverend Alison Schultz at Holy Innocents' Episcopal Church asked us to teach a memoir-writing class for the Holy Innocents' congregation in January 2014.

After agreeing to the request, we began a search for suitable material to guide the class. We reviewed many books on how to write memoirs and selected our favorite: William Zinsser's *Writing about Your Life*. By January we were ready to begin class meetings and encouraged the approximately twenty class members to read a chapter a week at home and to write a memoir each week during the class meeting. Each group met around a table and shared their efforts with each other, then chose one person to read aloud to the class.

At the end of May 2014 this class ended. But later in December 2014 a few members of the class were asked to read one of their memoirs for a holiday luncheon at the church. This event sparked renewed interest in writing memoirs, especially from some who had missed the first session. We agreed to start a new series of classes for those interested. Two of the members from the first class, Stefan Fatzinger and Christy Knight, wanted to continue. Beverly Baker (mother of Christy and a member of St. Philip's Cathedral), Tony Clarke, George Thomas, and Jeannie Longley joined during the two additional classes which also read another of Zinsser's books, *On Writing Well*, and wrote and read memoirs aloud. The classes ended in March of 2015. Later Janet Wilson joined this existing group.

The class evolved into a biweekly meeting throughout the year. All present, including the instructors, read a new or revised memoir for discussion. These meetings continued from 2015 until the day in March 2020 when the world closed down. After considering options for a few weeks, this dedicated group began to use Zoom to meet online weekly and have been doing so ever since.

Together our writing has improved, and our stories have evolved. The weekly meetings have become a sacred space for sharing our memoirs and personal histories, a place filled with light during these uncertain times. When our members began to think of publishing a collection of our memoirs, we looked to the help of Christy, who had just published a new novel, *On Display*, and Carolyn, a college faculty member who has published a book in her field, *Millennials Taking the Lead*, and the editing skills of Sally, a former college English professor. Now, this book has come to fruition.

We are grateful to all who have helped us on this journey, our families and friends, and Holy Innocents' Episcopal Church, especially the Reverend Bill Murray and the Reverend Martha Sterne, who now in official retirement has provided the introduction for us. We have decided in advance that any profits from book sales will be dedicated to the work of Holy Innocents'. And, we want to express many thanks to the current memoir writers: Beverly, Christy, Janet, Jeannie, Stefan, and Tony, all of whom continue to produce and share thoughtful and inspiring memoirs each week. It is our hope that these stories we've selected lift you and that they might encourage you to write a few memories of your life as well.

Dr. Carolyn Fore and Dr. Sally Parsonson

INTRODUCTION

Martha Sterne

A couple of years ago, I found a dusty manila folder in a dusty cardboard box under our bed and, lo and behold, in the six or seven typed pages in the folder, I found my father.

I think he was about my age (74) when he wrote these short bursts of childhood memories... the shady sidewalks on White Street; the railroad man who lived next door and took him for a train ride; his mother playing the piano, teaching piano; his doc father whistling on the way out the door with his bag; his quiet grandmother living with them; the sweetness of figs from the side yard tree; the three young boys he played with and the older tough boys they were scared of and ran from; the birth of an adored baby sister, her death from meningitis at six years old; his hatred of funerals; the daily comforts of kind people and fried chicken and plum jelly and butterbeans and pies.

Six or seven pages. A glimpse into another life became a glimpse into my own life. That is the gift of memoir. You don't just get to know the writer; you recognize yourself.

The great pleasure of the Holy Innocents' memoir meetings was always for me the glimpses of the people around the table through the wonder of memory and the beauty of the extraordinary in ordinary. Gifts that keep on giving.

I know you'll enjoy these pages and I hope you will dust off some memories of your own and write them down—maybe just in short bursts. Believe me. You are the keeper of treasures.

PART ONE

MAN WITH ONE PAIR OF SHOES

Sally Parsonson

One warm summer day when I was about eight years old, my father was driving my younger brother and me home to Greenville, Mississippi. We had visited his mother, my grandmother, in Grenada. Our un-air-conditioned car was not full this time, and I think my mother must have stayed at home with my baby sister while Peyton and I made the trip with him.

It was growing dark as we drove through the hills east of Greenwood when my father spotted a man in overalls walking along the side of the highway. He pulled off a safe distance ahead of the man and went back to speak to him. The two of them returned to the car. When the man got into the front seat next to my father, I noticed that he was barefoot and carrying a pair of heavy work shoes tied together by their shoelaces.

After a while, the man indicated to my father which dirt road to turn down off the highway, but other than that, there was no conversation. We bumped along the rough road until the man said, "Next turn-off, just stop. I can walk from there. It's too rutted to drive up."

So, my father stopped the car, and the man got out. He said, "Thank you very kindly, Mister. I really appreciate the lift."

We were almost back to the highway when my father noticed that the man's shoes were on the floor of the front seat. "We'll have to go back and leave his shoes," he said.

"Why?" Peyton and I both demanded. "Why take them back? They're just a dirty old pair of shoes. He probably won't care. We're hungry," we whined. "You said we could get hamburgers in Greenwood."

After he had turned the car around and headed back up the dusty road, my father said, "Never mind, we'll get there." When we arrived at the turn-off, the man was nowhere in sight. My father left the shoes hanging on a fence post.

As our father drove carefully in the dark back to the highway, Peyton and I pestered him again. "Why? Why'd we have to go back up that rough road just for an old, worn-out pair of shoes? They must've hurt his feet, or he wouldn't have been walking barefoot."

"Well," my father answered, "he was a country fellow, and in the country lots of folks go barefoot until they go to town. Those old shoes were probably the only ones he's ever had. I hope he finds them on that post.

He must not live too far up that road, so maybe he'll see them soon and know that we tried to do him right."

That silenced us, at least until we arrived at the hamburger place in Greenwood. But I have thought for a long time about the poor country man with his one worn-out pair of shoes and wondered if he ever found them again.

Now with my own closet full of too many shoes, I think not only of the man and his one pair but of my father's kindness to a stranger none of us would ever see again.

SERENDIPITY OR THE HOLY SPIRIT

Stefan Fatzinger

I have a scar on the side of my left upper thigh. It is about a foot long and looks like a railroad track with ties but with one of the tracks missing. It has been a part of me since I was twelve years old. I suppose that is why I haven't noticed it or paid any attention to it for several decades. We all have freckles, moles, bent noses, purple ankles, and other markers of our lives that are just a part of us and that we rarely if ever notice or think about. My scar is no different, but maybe it should be. There is a story to be told about that scar, and the small companion scar that resembles a small cross which I do notice occasionally, probably because its location is in my line of sight in the middle of my left thigh.

I was living in Elizabeth, New Jersey. Life was not pleasant. Regular beatings and, if we were fortunate, maybe one meal a day was "normal." But during the school year, there was at least escape from my purgatory for several hours during the day, which is probably why

I did so well in school at that point in my life, and I always had Sunday mornings to look forward to. That was when my friend and neighbor Russell and I would deliver the Sunday newspaper throughout Elizabeth.

We would be picked up at 5:00 a.m. by our boss Hank. Not only was this still the era of newspapers and young boys and girls earning money delivering those papers, but it was also the era of the station wagon, before the SUV. Hank's station wagon was a green Ford. In the back were bundles of the different sections of the Sunday papers—comics (always the outer layer), business section, gardening section, sports section, etc. Russell would sit in the back of the station wagon and put the various sections together into one paper and hand them to me, while I sat on the tailgate with my legs dangling down. When we arrived at an address, I would leap off the tailgate, distribute the papers on porches, lawns, or in mailboxes, and then jump back on the tailgate, receive another paper from Russell, and then turn around with my back to Russell and Hank, ready to leap off the tailgate for the next delivery. For the next three to four hours, Hank would drive, Russell would stuff, and I would deliver about two- or three-hundred Sunday papers. It was fun, and I enjoyed the work very much, even if I did have to give all my earnings to my stepmother.

On a Sunday in April 1960, the day would end a little differently from all the others. We had been delivering papers for approximately an hour. At this juncture in our route, we were on U.S. Highway 1, normally heavily traveled, but traffic was always light at 7:00 a.m. on a Sunday morning as the sky began to turn from black to gray in the early dawn. I had just delivered a paper and jumped back onto the tailgate but with my body twisted around to face Russell to receive another paper. Suddenly his eyes doubled or tripled in size, and he turned white as he screamed, "Watch out!" I snapped my head around to see a car about ten feet away approaching me at a speed of 30-40 miles per hour. I was mesmerized. It was like an out-of-body experience: I seemed to watch the next several seconds from above, as if watching a movie or television show. I felt no fear or anxiety in the split second before the car slammed into the rear of our station wagon and pushed it and me about twenty yards further down the highway. The driver of the vehicle had fallen asleep at the wheel, but the collision of the two cars jolted him awake. After the cars came to a stop, he came running out of his vehicle to discover his car on top of me. I was still sitting on the tailgate, which appeared to be unharmed, presumably because my body was between the two cars. Hank, frightened and shaken, had also gotten out of the station wagon and walked to the rear of his vehicle to join the driver of the car that had hit us. They both looked at me petrified, but at the time I didn't have a clue as to why. I was fine, or so I thought.

I didn't notice or realize that a car was sitting on top of me, but they did. The two of them, both large men, proceeded to lift the front end of the car off me and the tailgate.

Barely a minute or two later, or so it seemed to me, the police arrived. I have no idea how they became aware of the accident. Nevertheless, an officer was soon standing over me asking how I was. I advised him that I felt fine. And then I looked down. My left leg seemed as large as an elephant's. And there, protruding about ten or so inches out of my jeans was a large bone splinter that looked like the end of a spear. My jeans had been ripped by the compound fracture out of which I could observe blood pooling. I brought this to the attention of the police officer who immediately moved closer to me, lifted my head, and began hugging me so that I could not see my leg. The body's defense mechanisms are a marvelous manifestation of evolution. The accident had left me in shock; because of the shock, I felt no pain. As a matter of fact, my concerns were not of me, but of school, my brother and sisters, and what would happen next. I even asked Hank, Russell, and the driver of the other vehicle how they were, and remember chatting with the policeman about baseball. Then the ambulance arrived.

The EMTs approached me with a stretcher, but they had a problem. My body was in a sitting position. To be placed on a stretcher it would have to be in a prone position. My legs would have to be straightened. One EMT gently placed his arms under my left leg, an achievement since the leg appeared to be at least a yard in diameter. The other EMT grabbed my foot and thigh and pulled up and out. A crack like that of a rifle followed by a splintering sound like the shattering of a bat by a 95-mile-an-hour fastball filled the air, the sound so loud I think it could have been heard in New York City. And then my scream trumped the splintering sound. A pain unlike anything I had ever before or since experienced shot through my body. I passed out, awakening in the ambulance just as we arrived at the hospital. I would pass in and out of consciousness the rest of that day, presumably because of the pain medication.

It was evening when I fully regained my senses. I found myself in a hospital bed with my left leg wrapped in yards and yards of white gauze and hanging in the air, suspended there by pulleys and weights. I was in traction. I would remain in that position for four days while the doctors waited for the swelling to go down before operating. Following the operation that, unlike poor Humpty Dumpty, put my leg back together again, I awoke to find myself in a cast that began at the top of my chest and ran all the way down my left leg with only my toes showing and half-way down the right leg. A bar separated the two legs, and a hole had been cut around my groin area so that I could use a bedpan and urine bottle. This is how I would live for the next three months—in a hospital bed with most of my body covered in a cast. But it would be the best three months of my life between the ages of 10 and 15. Imagine, it took an automobile accident and a broken leg to find some happiness. For the first time in years I would eat three meals a day; I gained 20 pounds. And there was not a day during that period when I was beaten. As a matter of fact, I was surrounded by smiling nurses and orderlies, sweet candy-stripers, and a plethora of friends and well-wishers.

It was a sad day when I left the hospital on crutches late in July of 1960. However, I was now better able to cope with the nightmare that I limped back into when I got home after a three-month reprieve because of an incident that occurred during my second month in the hospital.

The day started out like all the others. I had finished breakfast, been washed, and had already flirted and laughed with the nurses and candy-stripers. It was about 10:00 a.m. Suddenly my entire being was bathed in a feeling of peace and love. It was as if there was another human standing beside me or more accurately another presence. I didn't fight the sensation nor even ponder what was happening to me. I simply enjoyed the experience. And then, for no reason that I can explain, I picked up the Gideon Bible that was in the drawer of the stand next to my bed and began reading. Remember,

I was twelve. I had never in my life to that point read a Bible nor felt the need to do so. I read peacefully for the rest of the day. My roommate, nurses, and other visitors questioned my behavior. I had no response to their queries other than to shrug my shoulders, smile, and continue reading. Little did I know that I was in the presence of God.

The next day I woke normally, and life resumed as if the day before had never happened. I didn't give it a second thought until my minister from the Moravian Church visited me three days later. During his visit, he asked me whether anything unusual had occurred on Tuesday. He went on to explain that all the children in Vacation Bible School had prayed for me on that day at approximately 10:00 a.m., some saying that they saw God visiting me. Tuesday was three days earlier, but I had already forgotten about my experience and answered his question with "no, I don't think so." It was only after my minister left that my roommate, having heard our conversation, reminded me that I had read the Bible all day on Tuesday. The lightbulb lit; I had an epiphany. At that moment I knew that I had met God and that God exists. From that day forward, I have often returned to this memory when troubled or in doubt. I also have the scars on my leg to remind me.

THE HERSHEY BAR

Carolyn Fore

We moved from Lake Charles, Louisiana to Pittsburgh, Pennsylvania when I was in the third grade. I found I needed to adapt to many changes at my new school as I quickly realized that being a southern girl in this northern city was quite a culture shock. Fortunately, most of my classmates thought it was cute when I said "picture show" instead of "movie theater" and referred to them as "y'all," but I still felt self-conscious about being different.

I preferred to take my lunch from home instead of eating the school cafeteria lunches which often contained food items I wasn't familiar with. My mother packed the exact same lunch for me every day, so I was surprised when I opened my lunchbox one day and the usual Hershey Bar wasn't there. After school I asked my mother about it, and she said she had put the candy bar in my lunchbox that morning when she packed my lunch.

The next day when I got ready to eat lunch, the candy bar was missing again. This continued for about a week before she and I became annoyed and felt we needed to figure out what was happening. I explained to my mother that I didn't dare report it to my gruff teacher because she wasn't very friendly to me, and I didn't think she would be sympathetic about my missing Hershey Bar.

The next morning as my mother handed me my lunchbox she said, "If your Hershey Bar is still in your lunchbox at lunch time, don't eat it. I'll explain later." I was puzzled but agreed. At lunch time I opened my lunchbox, and my Hershey Bar was missing again, as I expected.

That afternoon in the girls' bathroom, the pudgy girl in the class came up to me and said, "It's a good thing for you that you didn't eat your Hershey Bar today because something was wrong with it. I had to throw it out." Shocked by her confession, I simply looked at her in disbelief as she walked away.

When I got home from school, I told my mother who explained to me that she melted the Hershey Bar just a little and put pepper on the bottom of it then let it get hard again in the refrigerator and wrapped it back up perfectly. The two of us laughed until we had tears, and my Hershey Bar was never stolen from my lunchbox again.

THE SILVER SADDLE MOUNTAIN GANG

Beverly Baker

I don't know exactly what triggered my memories about the Silver Saddle Mountain Gang. Maybe it was the toy six-guns I saw the other day while browsing in an antique shop. The guns were not child-sized. They seemed larger than life to me and were housed in beautifully crafted holsters. Seeing them reminded me of the time the kid downstairs (I think his name was Michael Brick) tried to knock my brother out with one of those, just like in a Hopalong Cassidy movie. Luckily, Mom was watching us from the upstairs window. She screamed, and the villain dropped his weapon.

In the shop, the guns were displayed on a long table with other Western items: hats, spurs, saddle bags, and the most elaborately-tooled leather saddle I've ever seen. At one end of the table was a staged group of lead Cowboy and Indian toys engaged in their usual antics. But most exciting to me was a stack of well-worn vintage Western story books for young readers. Once upon a time, I had read all of them.

When I think about the Silver Saddle Mountain Gang, as we nicknamed it, I realize how much fun I had as a child and how much I adored my brother for inviting me into the gang—a girl and a few years older. We grew up during the heyday of the American Cowboy and Indian mania. Everybody was obsessed with it. Maybe it was the first manifestation of the mind-controlling media in modern life. After school we would listen to the cowboy shows on the radio. Mom would set up cookies and milk. The anticipation was enormous as we dropped our school sacks down and prepared to listen. There is something about radio stories that engages the mind in a special way. The insistent visual world that dominates us so thoroughly now is relegated to the background. We are left with only our ears and have to rely upon our imaginations to "see" what we are listening to.

But it would only be a matter of time before our imaginative radio experience would be transformed by television when Dad came home with the first neighborhood TV. Whoa! It was a big-status event even though the screen measured only seven inches. No matter. It was major, and our radio heroes were suddenly rendered into their Hollywood incarnations. There and then we were transported to the cinematic and ultimately digital future for better or worse.

We didn't think about any of this at the time. Our job was to ride to Silver Saddle Mountain every Saturday. I remember all the members of our posse would don cowboy gear and head out for the shootout. Our costumes were very important. We had Western holsters and guns that to me in retrospect were like actual six-shooters, made to scale but for children. We looked like cowboy dwarfs. Some of these faux weapons were cap guns which made them seem more real, more exciting to pretend with.

Our bikes were our horses. We rode in a pack and shouted slang cowboy phrases all the while headed for Silver Saddle Mountain. Actually, the mountain was a twenty-foot-high bulldozed cliff carved out of the old cemetery hill behind our building. We called the cemetery "Tombstone." We staged battles among the graves.

Except for a man who was probably the caretaker, I don't recall seeing any visitors to the old, neglected place. He went about his chores and didn't pay any attention to us. But one day the school bully appeared with his gang. They were not wearing cowboy gear, they were older, and to me they were scary.

They began to taunt us with insulting language—particularly me, the only girl. I was a little older, closer to their age. Sometimes in a situation like this when the scent of fear fills the air, a collective decision is made unwittingly. We decided in an unspoken way to run for our bikes and beat it out of there, all the while knowing that something had changed.

Our game born out of an enthusiastic, even obsessive, brand-new devotion to everything Western which had come to us over the modern wires like something magical, like some fantastic destiny-driven thing, had made us imagine ourselves actual movie cowboys— almost.

But now the Silver Saddle Mountain Gang had a real enemy in real time—a real outlaw in the game. His name was John Pew. He had been to reform school. Our parents would refer to him as a bad example. They would say, "You see, this is what happens to kids who don't behave."

Later that night, my brother and I were quiet at dinner. We had made it down the mountain and had dodged their zinging rocks. Our mom, who talked all the time even to herself, said, "Cat got your tongues?" I was hesitant, but I knew I had to tell her. "We saw that Pew boy on Silver Saddle today. He's scary." Mom looked worried. "Don't have anything to do with him. He's a bad boy."

It was one of those moments between parents and children. Mom was right, yet there was a challenge floating around, hovering over the table along with the tombstones whirling around in our minds from the day's experience. My brother and I exchanged a look.

Our horses were at rest in the garage. Kids will just be kids.

The next Saturday came around. Our gang met as usual dressed for our wild-west game. We started out with an enthusiastic cowboy roar, all whoops and hee-haws, while waving our guns and shooting. My brother had a new pack of extra loud rolls of caps—positively deafening! We rode our horses (bikes) up the steep mountain until it just got too tough. We dismounted and lugged our bikes up over the top, finally reaching the solemn level ground of Tombstone.

Up there everything was exhilarating even though it was a repository of death. But death to us was only some other fiction in our repertoire of amusements. That day was a perfect spring day, breezy, full of blooms and action.

At first, we didn't see them or hear them. Then a rock zinged by my head. John Pew was about ten yards away leering at me. I began to feel fear in blotches breaking out around my neck. I saw my little brother and friends standing near me, motionless, looking at Pew and his gang of two. We had seven. I quickly moved behind a tree.

I suddenly realized the others, my gang, backed up toward me as though seeking shelter. Pew threw another rock. It too missed. I braced myself against what I now call my lucky tree. And since I was the big sister, I suddenly felt like the babysitter. Pew started shouting curses at me. I shuddered. I was not used to being bullied. Then within an instant, an urge came upon me. I yelled, "Pew!" as loud as I could in my most authoritative eight-year-old voice. Pew jerked his head and squinted his eyes at me. He looked like a pig. I had to suppress a weird urge to laugh. It was one of those insanely detached moments in time. I couldn't help myself. I looked at him and inched away from my sheltering tree. Then I boldly held my nose and shouted, "Something stinks!" That was the trigger. He started groping around for rocks, but his two buddies just stood there, befuddled, looking at me. Pew sensed it was him against me. He lunged at me. I caught a flash of bright metal in his outstretched hand. I was terrified. I saw my brother, Sammy, throw a rock at him and scream something. Pew hesitated as though deciding which one of us to go for first.

But in the next moment a horn sounded and a man in a uniform stepped out of a big black van—was it a hearse? I don't really remember, but he scolded us saying that we were trespassing on cemetery property. His voice boomed over the tombstones like an angry god of the dead. "I'm calling the police to come and arrest you—all of you!" I saw Pew make a hasty retreat from whence he came. The Silver Saddle Mountain Gang did likewise.

I've always wondered if Mom had called the cemetery caretaker whom she had spoken to a couple of times.

Afterwards, safely at home, I asked her about it. A puzzled expression came over her face. It was as though she hadn't heard the question, and I realized she hadn't asked me about Tombstone the way she usually did when we came back on Saturday afternoons. Instead, she said that she and Mrs. Fox, my best girl friend's mother, had arranged ballet lessons for us on Saturday afternoons. "I'm so excited about this" she gushed. "In fact, I have a present for you."

She handed over the big pink box. It looked expensive. It was wrapped and embellished with pink satin ribbons. Somehow, I knew it was not going to be the hand-tooled leather cowgirl belt I was hoping to get for my birthday. I felt peculiar as I began to peel away the ribbons and layers of gauzy pink tissue paper. There it was before me in all of its contrived splendor like an omen or a messenger from charm school. It was the most beautiful Madame Alexander ballerina doll. Her hair was auburn, piled in curls on her head. Her pink tutu, a bit of rosy fluff, was attached to an exquisite satin bodice which mirrored the exacting nature of her accurately crafted pink satin ballet slippers—those instruments of torture.

Yet, to this day, pink satin ballet slippers hold a special mystique for me. After all, they did impart the knowledge that I had two left feet and would never be a ballerina. And where was my new doll's cowgirl hat and her big pearl-handled six-gun, not to mention the hand-tooled holster? What kind of a gift was this anyway? How would I explain this dancer doll to my collection of lead Cowboy and Indian toys?

What I did understand on that day in 1948 was that my identity color as a female would be pink—WAIT, not so fast podna. Color is blind. Color exists only in the eye of the beholder and today, right now, I feel turquoise. My ball cap, my shirt, and most definitely, my desire to have the hand-tooled turquoise buckled belt of my dreams which would confirm my cowgirl experience. Actually, the experience is the dreaming part. Cervantes was right. However befuddling, it is the dreams that continually invade our consciousness and guide us that help us to survive. Viva! —the remembered dream game of the Silver Saddle Mountain Gang.

Editors' note: This memoir was originally written as a letter from Bev to her brother, Sammy. It included the following text:

Dear Sammy,

I have been thinking about you. I had such a lovely time with your daughter, Samara, at Mom's 95th birthday party in New Jersey. Samara looks and acts like a Botticelli angel. Perhaps that is her mother's Italian heritage shining through. Anyway, I told her that I was writing memoir stories and thought you might enjoy reading one that is about an adventure we had as children. She thought you would.

Love, Bev

P.S. What's that phrase about anything related to real people is not intentional? So I have gathered my thoughts and created a story from bits and pieces of my memory. It would be fun to hear what you remember about Silver Saddle.

UNHEARD BIRDS

Christy Baker Knight

The day the School for the Deaf buses pull up to Emma Wetlands, the sky is soft, autumn gray in the 60s with a hum of crickets only some can hear. The theme they've chosen for their field trip is Birds, and the wonders of teaching a subject so vast and colorful without using our sense of hearing has consumed our team as we've overprepared by learning signs for: hi, welcome, bird, look, draw, nest, build.

We meet our group at the Emma Lane bridge which accesses acres of wetlands behind a residential cul-de-sac named after the wife of a once-landowner. It's an urban environment that carries the rush of highway background in winter, but in October is still cushioned by deciduous leaves the trees haven't yet lost to the season. Being here feels like stepping back in time to the Atlanta of my childhood: backyards with no fences woven together into a blanket of English ivy under tall trees, an ochre yellow thread of creek running through the dark green; heart-shaped tracks in the mud left by grazing deer; lavender aster and yellow goldenrod clinging to their stalks amid scarlet dogwood berries and leaves, creating a vivid tapestry.

We divide the students whose ages range widely into four color teams as requested, each naturalist with a flag on our backpacks that they will follow. Mine is as yellow as the tulip poplar leaves that scatter our path. I pray that I'm doing the basic greeting signs right. The interpreter helps and relaxes my worries. I'm projecting my voice differently, realizing that if we want to see birds, we might have the best chance of doing so with this quiet group. Most field trips are so loud that by the time we get to the more secret places at Emma, we've scared everything away.

But they do have questions, and the interpreter fires them at me. What is the red bird called? Does it live here? How do birds hide? Are we going to see a Great Blue Heron here at Blue Heron Nature Preserve?

A chattering Nuthatch gets my attention, and I point for them to see where it is walking upside down on a tree. An older child locks onto it and grunts for others to find it too. My expectation of this being a quiet group changes as I learn that working with children who have hearing loss is a louder experience than you'd think. There is a lot of shouting and smacking that accompanies the movement of hands, and a need to express themselves. The varying degrees of loss make for a range of communication levels; some children can hear my words, and some can only understand the signing of the interpreter.

An occasional blip from our walkie talkies helps move the groups along in time to visit all the stations: observing with binoculars, nest building, drawing and field sketching, and seeing different habitats for birds. I'm thrilled that we can explore the subject in depth, carry the words into deeper territory, consume the colors of common backyard birds in a fun fan guide that I carry. They lunge for it, hungry for visuals. What we can't hear, we are going to see to the full extent.

Enthusiasm lifts us like no other program I've experienced before: delight in each discovery, an urgency of experiencing all we can. They take turns with binoculars, drawing materials, and field guides. They build nests of their own using pine straw, moss, and sticks they gather. They form tiny eggs out of clay. My strengths as an art teacher come in handy as I demonstrate a way to make field sketches. Then they wow me with their drawing skills. Once immersed in their projects, the hum of activity seems to draw the birds to us as I live the mantra, "We learn most when we are teaching." A heron stands still as a statue out in the water beyond our picnic tables.

ON SEEING BILLY GRAHAM

Tony Clarke

Our family moved from Cleveland, Ohio, and eventually ended up in Columbia, Kentucky, in 1947. I found myself in this small town fascinated by visiting evangelical preachers, especially those conducting revival meetings. Those preachers, usually men, were generally well dressed, articulate, charismatic, and brought intriguing messages, sometimes angry and sometimes compelling with what they portrayed as the ultimate answer to life itself. Looking back, I realized that maybe not only was I finding these evangelical preachers entertaining, but I was at the beginning of my own quest for some answers on the bigger questions in life.

In the fall of 1949, as a sophomore at Harvard College, I was delighted to hear that Billy Graham, one of that period's most important names in the preaching field, was coming to Mechanics Hall, a convention venue in Boston, for big crowds. I wanted to hear him, but also wanted to have some company on the venture. As luck would have it, my only roommate around, out of the four of us, was Harold Brown, a devout Roman Catholic. When I asked if he would go with me, Harold refused to have anything to do with it. "I'm Catholic you know, and we are not permitted to participate in any other religious services outside of our own." Then he added, "I could be excommunicated, and that's a fate worse than death." However, after much conversation and lots of ardent persuasion, I got Harold to agree to go as long as we only watched the proceeding and didn't participate. Since that was my intent, too, he consented reluctantly.

Mechanics Hall was filled with people, all bubbling with excitement, and we quickly took our seats. The service opened with some outstanding music by George Beverly Shea, Graham's longtime associate. This music was designed to put the crowd in a happy, receptive frame of mind and ready to embrace Billy Graham's stirring message of faith and redemption. The music was marvelous, and I felt myself falling into that mood of bliss and openness to the magic of this event.

Then Billy Graham strode onto the stage, tall, slender, handsome, immaculately dressed, and focused on his purpose for the afternoon. He paced like a lion from one side of the stage to the other, his voice ranging from a high compelling tone to a low forceful ring of authority as to our purpose in the world, joining God in a quest for goodness and faith. I was mesmerized, or maybe hypnotized like Mowgli in Walt Disney's *Jungle Book* by that wily snake (who kept lisping "Trusssssss me") and falling into a state of abandonment of my critical sense. Harold, on the other hand, was sitting there with eyes wide open like a deer in headlights. But Billy Graham kept going on with a passionate summons to each person to be saved by God's everlasting grace.

Finally, when Billy Graham was finished, and smiling, he exhorted each person to come down front and learn more about the pathway to God's eternal love and freedom from fear and doubt through acceptance of the grace of Jesus. I looked at Harold and said, "Let's go down and see what they do. We don't have to agree to anything. We will just go down and see how they handle this." Harold stared at me with a look of fear and disbelief as if I had suggested we jump into the icy waters of Boston Harbor. I tried to explain to him again we weren't going to do anything or sign anything but see what they do. Harold quickly pointed out again for the tenth time, "I can't do that. I am Catholic, and the Pope will excommunicate me for even thinking about it."

In the seats in front of us was a family of seven; Mom, Dad, with their Bibles, and five children who were attentively watching the father and mother. The father turned around to Harold, having overheard our conversation, looked him straight in the eye, and said

"You need to go down, son." I almost burst out laughing, but Harold turned to me with a bewildered look and said after much hesitation, "All right. I'll go, but I'm not promising or signing anything." I think Harold had felt that this man might pick him up and carry him down.

So off we went, with about a third of the audience, to the front where we were ushered downstairs in groups of about fifteen or so into individual conference rooms. There we were met by either seminary students or ministers who talked briefly to us and picked up names, addresses, and telephone numbers. I never knew until years later that Harold had given them the name and phone number of our other roommate, Bob Chase, who had frequently asked why a local Baptist Church kept calling him.

I learned a lot about Harold, his truly ardent faith, and the intent to practice it fully. I very much liked Harold, who was a good student and friend. Always gracious, he enjoyed a good time and participated in our raucous parties. He dated, off and on, the granddaughter of the publisher of the Boston Post, a local daily newspaper. We always thought Harold might end up with Mary Grozier, the granddaughter, but that never happened. He taught science at a prestigious Connecticut prep school, The Choate School, which John F. Kennedy attended. Harold was an outstanding teacher.

Although Harold has since died, his memory will always be with us. He was a fine individual, true friend, and someone we cherished greatly. I'll always remember his gift to me as a companion to see Billy Graham.

THE CALCULUS WAS CORRECT

Jeannie Longley

I arrived at Wellesley College in the fall of 1973, coming from a medium-sized midwestern town, and having attended a not-very-good high school. Most of the women at Wellesley had either attended private secondary schools or came from better public high schools than mine. I didn't know what the initials "AP" stood for because my high school didn't have any advanced-placement courses. After my junior year in high school when I had taken trigonometry, there were no other math courses to take, so a friend and I did "independent study," which basically meant we chatted for those 50 minutes. When I started college, I felt woefully unprepared, and the first few semesters were tough.

I had decided in high school that I wanted to go to medical school and realized right off the bat that this was going to be a tall order. So I buckled down and worked hard in my classes, harder than most of my new friends. Although I had originally planned to major in one of the sciences, I quickly decided that I didn't really want to be in the middle of all of those competitive women. Liberal arts were not my strong suit, so I chose math as a major. At a small school, the focus was primarily on theoretical math. I loved the elegant proofs and theorems, and I loved solving problems. It was also black and white, and for most problems, there was just one solution: I liked this as well.

I dated in college and had some boyfriends, but my primary focus was my studies. I did take some literature, art, and photography classes my senior year of college, and found that not only did I really enjoy them, but I could attain decent grades. Early in the second semester of my senior year, I had already been accepted to a few medical schools, so my plans were set. I was heading back to the Midwest.

One evening I began chatting with the girl who lived across the hall from me, and she had the idea of fixing me up on a date with her boyfriend's roommate. Her boyfriend was a junior at MIT, and his apartment mate was a math PhD graduate student at MIT. Two math nerds—it was a match made in heaven, or so she thought. I was impressed by his awesome-sounding name which ended with "the Third." Plans were made for us to meet at the apartment in Cambridge, where my friend and her boyfriend would cook dinner. It was a total flop. We did not connect, and he wanted to go over to see the Hasty Pudding Club performance after dinner. So, after an awkward meal, we parted ways.

I stayed for a time at the apartment with my friend and her boyfriend, and, as luck would have it, one of his other friends, an electrical engineering/computer science major, happened by the apartment. I will never forget seeing him walk in, because, although he looked like he was about 12 years old, he walked in wearing a trench coat and smoking a pipe. His name was Lester Longley. The four of us spent the rest of the evening chatting and laughing, with no expectations at all. He was all excited about his new TI graphing calculator. We ended up making jokes that we thought were hilarious double entendres, but were not really all that clever. Some examples:

Have you ever seen a truck tire?

Have you ever heard a diamond ring?

Have you ever seen a bell hop?

Have you ever seen a cactus pair?

And so on. Eventually it got late, and this very young-looking man walked me to my car. I didn't think I would ever see him again, but he was so warm and courteous that when he called a few weeks later to invite me to dinner and a concert, I accepted. We ended up seeing each other once a week or so for my remaining few months of college, but with no expectations beyond that. On our second date, I told him that I did not plan to marry, ever. We did have lots of phone conversations and really enjoyed each other's company. But I was headed to medical school, and he had another year as an undergraduate, hoping to go on to Berkeley to pursue engineering. I did, however, invite him to my graduation and to dinner with my parents. He surprised me with a lovely silver-and-pearl bracelet from Shreve, Crump and Low. When my mother saw it, she said, "That's an awfully nice gift for a transient boyfriend!" Late that night, we bid our *adieus*, with no plans to see each other again. But we did talk on the phone, and when he invited me to visit him at his home in Chattanooga, I accepted. The rest is history, and the math added up.

ONE NIGHT IN JULY

Janet Wilson

A quick glance at the digital clock centered on the well-lit dashboard showed the time to be 11:15 p.m. We had just enjoyed dinner at Dad's favorite Italian restaurant in Indian Harbour Beach.

"Anyone interested in stopping for a walk along the beach before heading home?"

"It's late; I'm tired," Gail moaned.

"Ow, my sunburn! Not a chance," my other sister complained. Three hours on the beach at the hottest part of the day and she had never reapplied her sunscreen.

I was disappointed, yet not at all ready to forget the idea on this last night of our stay at Dad's. I tried once more. "Tomorrow we fly back to New York. This is our last opportunity to see them. Wouldn't it be fantastic if we could see them and tell the kids all about it when we get home?"

We had met an elderly man on the beach earlier that evening who had retired from the US Air Force. Dad had served in the Navy. The two got to talking and their conversation led to his telling about having seen a loggerhead turtle at this beach the previous night. I reminded my sisters of this. "That doesn't mean we'll see one tonight," whined Diane. "Maybe next year, Janet."

My last hope rested with Dad who remained silent, and the silence continued until he pulled into his parking spot, number 19. I could feel the waves of my excitement crashing into instant disappointment. As we climbed the four flights of steps, the only sounds I heard were the groans of my two sisters, one tired and the other suffering discomfort, and the shuffle of our sandals.

We entered Dad's condo unit and as Dad placed his keys on the little wicker shelf hanging in the entry hallway, he turned to me saying, "Just give me a minute to change out of this white outfit and I'll go down to the beach with you."

I was filled with immense joy. My dad wanted to do this with me and for me. I was a grown woman with three children of my own, yet, at that moment a depth of appreciation filled me, healing an emptiness I had not realized was there. There had been few times in my life that I had truly felt Dad's genuine wanting to make the effort to be with me and share in something that mattered to me. I do remember once when our family went to the railroad picnics at Croton Point Park and I got to be Dad's partner in the egg-toss contest. We did pretty well; I felt proud, but we didn't win. I remember the times that Dad would throw the softball with me in a game of catch. When he threw the ball really high into the air, I was always nervous it would come down and hit me in the face. I wish that it had been Dad's confidence in my ability to handle the ball that helped me overcome my fear, but I don't remember being particularly encouraged. I think I felt it was more like a challenge given, a need for me to do it for him. When I graduated from high school, I got an award I had not known I was going to receive. It was the Best All Around Girl Athlete award. I was surprised and thrilled... until I heard my dad say, "That's my boy." Dad had wanted a son. He got three daughters. I was most like the son he never had. I felt the bubble of joy deflate. I knew I was a good athlete, but I also knew that there were at least two others who were more talented athletes than I was, so I felt I didn't really deserve the award. Years later, when I questioned my dad about why the Rotary gave me the award instead of giving it to Pattie or Margaret, he couldn't give me an answer, but I surmised that he had somehow had a hand in it.

I learned how to use a mitt properly at the summer recreation day camp in town. And years later I became an excellent third-base player for a women's team in

Yorktown Heights. Overcoming that fear also helped me to become a good basketball player. I just wish Dad had come to my games. The only basketball game I remember him coming to was at Cardinal Hayes in the Bronx when the CYO girls' basketball team I played with made it to the sectional playoff. Both Mom and Dad came to see the game, but only because we were going to the Bronx anyway; we visited with my grandparents at least every other weekend. I was so nervous I took only one shot while I was on the court, and I didn't make the basket. Dad did come to a women's softball game once. My sister and I played for the same team. I was sure he was only there to see her play.

I do remember feeling happy on Sunday afternoons when Dad and I stayed indoors and watched the New York Giants football games on television. Unfortunately, I remember Dad always shushing me, saying, "Stop asking so many questions and watch the game."

I thought, "I am watching, and I really want to understand. Why did they call a penalty? Why did they decide to kick the ball rather than pass it? What does that referee's signal mean?" I really did question, comment, shout, and feel excitement watching the games. I loved that I was watching them with Dad. Maybe he did like having me watch with him but just didn't know how to let me know that.

So, on that evening I could hardly contain my excitement at the possibility of seeing the loggerhead turtles. I had first read about loggerheads in a GEO magazine article written by a retired policeman who had become involved in protecting and saving them.

Within minutes we were on our way. Conversations with "watchers" camped along the dunes continued to echo through my mind. Mounting expectation wanted to burst into realization. The exquisite light of the night's moon beckoned these sea creatures to surface and come onto the beach.

It was July 8, 1984, and throughout the month hundreds of loggerhead turtles would journey to the dunes of Sebastian Beach and Satellite Beach once again. Dad and I, with flashlights in hand, began our walk. As numerous sand crabs scurried in and out of the moonlight, our imaginations danced amidst the shadows. I really wanted to see a loggerhead turtle emerge from the sea, coming ashore to lay her eggs! I was filled with anticipation, wondering where we would see her, how large would she be, what evidence there would be of her movement from the shore to the dunes, how she would find the just right spot for her nest....

Suddenly, Dad said, "Look. There are your tracks, Jan." Sure enough there they were, deep marks in the sand left as she had pulled her weight forward and created a path to the place she would dig her nest.

"Dad, I had no idea what her path would look like; it's amazing. I am almost overwhelmed by the thrill of seeing this for the first time and I haven't even seen the turtle!" I sang out to him.

"Yes, but there are two sets of tracks, Jan. One was left as the loggerhead made her way up to the dunes; the other was left when she went back to the sea." My heart sank as I realized I would not see this giant sea creature after all. Almost at once, my mind's eye started to show me images of what had taken place only a short while before we had arrived at this spot on the beach.

As she dragged herself across the sand, she had created a deep track with flipper markings on the outer edges. For the turtle, probably weighing nearly three hundred and fifty pounds, making her way to the dunes had been slow and arduous. There she had entrusted to Nature the safety of her eggs, as many as two hundred of them. Upon reaching the dunes she had dug a narrow nest, then dropped the soft-shelled eggs into it. Next she had covered them with sand by using her mighty flippers. She could not know or understand that the natural dunes no longer provided sufficient protection for her offspring.

Many of her eggs would not survive the two months until their hatching date; they would be crushed by the now all-too-common bulldozers of progress. As her hatchlings emerged from their sand-filled nest, they would be fooled into thinking they were following the light of the moon as they struggled to make their way to the sea. Instead of following the reflected light off the sea, these helpless babies would move toward the glowing, glittery lights of newly constructed hotels and condominiums, pools, and parking lots. They would move further away from their life-sustaining sea environment to almost certain death.

Having carefully covered her eggs, the female turtle had turned, leaving her nest to begin pulling herself back through the sand down to the shore, creating a second track parallel to the first, about fourteen and a half feet from it. She had completed her journey on reentering the sea where much like an expectant father, her mate would have anxiously awaited the forty-five minutes or so that it had taken for her to complete her life-giving work. She would never again return to her nest.

I looked toward the sea and there flickering in the moonlight I imagined this extraordinary couple swimming off home—into the depths of darkness. "Perhaps Dad and I will see loggerheads come ashore and lay their eggs next year," I thought. Then I realized Dad was talking to me: "Jan, you'll have to come down and see me next year so we can walk the beach together. Depending on when you come, we can see a loggerhead turtle or two, maybe more and...maybe we will even see hatchlings make their way to the sea." An invitation to spend more time together...a perfect ending to this visit with Dad.

PART TWO

The Wardrobe

Carolyn Fore

When I look across my den at the stately piece of furniture I refer to as "the wardrobe" that now contains an assortment of treasures, including old VHS tapes of my daughter's cheerleading competitions, miscellaneous tablecloths for holidays, and directories from a variety of organizations, I often think of the long history of this oversized family heirloom.

I first remember it standing against the wall in my grandmother's bedroom. It seemed magical, as did most of her things in my young imagination. She kept her clothes hanging in this wardrobe, those items consisting mostly of cotton flowery shirtwaist dresses. Some of those dresses were for wearing around the house, and others were fancier for special occasions. But as I recall, she basically wore the same dress every day, and they all came from that wardrobe.

After my grandmother died in 1978 at the age of 101, my mother shipped a lot of her furniture and other items from Luling, Texas to Augusta, Georgia. There were quite a few pieces of furniture, but the large wardrobe was the most difficult item to ship since it is just under eight feet tall, four feet wide, and three feet deep. It ended up in storage for a few years until my parents built an addition to their residence that included a new master suite with high ceilings. The wardrobe was cleaned up and had a nice new home where my mother could enjoy its elegance and memories.

A few years after my father's death in 1992, my mother sold their house and moved to a condo that didn't have space for the wardrobe. She offered it to me, so Tom and I figured out how to put it, along with some other items she had to get rid of, in a U-Haul and bring them to Atlanta. But we didn't have a good place for the wardrobe in our residence. The only room with tall ceilings didn't have an open wall where we could put such a large piece of furniture, so we decided it would go in our storage room for a while. That presented another problem. The storage room was over the garage with an outside entrance at the top of a staircase. There was no way to carry the wardrobe up the stairs then turn it to go in the small door opening to the storage room. Finally, Tom figured out a way to create a pulley with ropes to hoist it up from the ground, over the railing at the top of the stairs, and straight into the storage room. With the help of both of our teenage sons, he managed to get it tucked away in the storage room for safekeeping.

About five years later we sold the house and moved to a larger one that had a living room with a high ceiling that I felt would be a perfect place for the wardrobe. However, it had been moved around and stored so it needed to be refinished before it would be presentable as a key piece of living room furniture. I found a furniture guy who restored antique pieces and came up with a plan. He would pick it up at the old house, refinish it, and deliver it to our new location. That helped us with the moving problem. I scheduled a pickup date with him before our move date and Tom got the boys to help him one Sunday afternoon so he could reverse the rope and pulley process he used to get the wardrobe upstairs to the storage room to get it back down. They almost knocked the entire railing off the stairway and nearly dropped the wardrobe onto the ground in the process but managed to get it back downstairs and put it in the garage to be picked up. The next day the furniture guy came, and I showed him the piece. He admired it and said he would be glad to take it and return it finished to the new address. I asked, "How can you do that? You came by yourself in a pickup truck." He said, "Easy, watch me. This piece is from the 1800s and was built for a wagon train. I can tell from the design that the top was added or replaced in the early 1900s. It can be taken apart and folded up." I said,

"Oh my, wait until my husband and my mother hear that. They have both spent a lot of money and effort moving it around just like it is!" He showed me how it could be disassembled and folded flat after the top piece was taken off and the body was removed from the base. But that wasn't the end the story.

These events happened in November of 1999, and we moved the weekend before Thanksgiving. I waited months for the refinisher to call to tell me he was ready to deliver the completed wardrobe. A couple of times I called him, and he said he was getting to it. Finally, I called him to say that we were having a family reunion at our house over the Fourth of July weekend, and I needed to have it by then. He said, "Well, I have been meaning to ask you if you want me to patch this hole that was in the drawer in the base. You probably remember that we talked about it when I picked it up and decided it wasn't a keyhole but couldn't figure out what it was. I can fill it in." I told him to go ahead and fill it in.

A few weeks later my mother called me from Texas. She was visiting her brothers and stopped by to visit a second cousin. They started talking about family history, and the cousin said, "You know I have the gun that belonged to our grandfather, John Kelsey Moore from Galveston." He was the founder of the first newspaper in The Republic of Texas, *The Civilian* in 1833. She went on to say, "He accidentally shot the gun inside the house and missed hitting anyone but shot a hole in the wardrobe. Later your mother ended up with the wardrobe, and I was wondering what has happened to it." When my mother told her that I had it and it was being refinished, they both decided the bullet hole needed to stay so she called to tell me. I quickly called the furniture refinisher to ask if he had filled it in yet, and he sheepishly said no. I was relieved to hear that he still hadn't finished and said, "Then don't do it. I want to leave that hole since it has a family story behind it and a cousin still has the gun that shot the bullet that made the hole." So, he left the hole and finished the work, getting the wardrobe back to me just in time for the family reunion. I moved the wardrobe one more time to my current residence, but this time when the movers I hired arrived, I showed them how to take the wardrobe apart before moving it.

ABOVE THE LIBRARY

Christy Baker Knight

I n the fall of 2001, several events happened that would test us as a nation as well as a family. I learned that Art could be more than a calling for me, to trust in its refuge, a lofty place among leaves.

I spent those days perched on scaffolding above voracious readers in the children's area of the Roswell Library. Almost two years before, I'd been awarded a commission to produce a mural there, and because Fulton County funds ran as slow as molasses, by the time they were released to begin the work, my husband Michael and I had nested and hatched a baby.

The mural was of two beloved children's stories: "The Owl and the Pussycat" and *The Secret Garden*. I'd created a scaled cartoon of the mural and won the award because I turned the existing round window in the space into a sun and moon. Not only was it a wonderful opportunity to inspire children to read, the pay for the job was good income for a freelance artist.

I rented scaffolding and hired painters to make the base coats for the night and day sides of the mural. I never could have stayed on budget without Mom and Dad's free childcare. Several mornings a week, I'd drop ten-month-old Baby Bev off at their home and then hit the highway for the twenty-minute commute. Surrounded by the library's treasure trove of audio books, I listened to stories and got lost in the brushwork of feathers in the owl and the little bird that showed the way to the secret garden. I included the Georgia State Bird, the Brown Thrasher, in rust and cream. Lois Lowry, Daphne Du Maurier, Edith Wharton, and other authors kept me going with deep and often heart-wrenching stories.

In the middle of the project, 9/11 happened. The days spent before it working in a public building and the days after were markedly different. The jovial air of families selecting books had been replaced by a silence beyond the typical library shushing. Then, two things happened in our family. First my take-charge mother-in-law started getting lost when driving to visit us from her home in western North Carolina, a trip she'd taken dozens of times. She stopped talking in her usual friendly tone and was quiet, lost-looking, as she developed a rapid onset of Alzheimer's. Granny Phyllis had worked in a library, too. I had visited the high school where she'd recently retired from a long career as a beloved librarian, coach, and mentor surrounded by a gaggle of friends.

Then, just as Michael and his dad were coping with this mournful new reality, Baby Bev turned one. We took her to the doctor for a checkup, and he noticed a heart murmur. He said not to worry but to get a second opinion. That test happened the day of a plane crash over Long Island when a community full of 9/11 first responders lost even more lives. Michael and I held our breath as we watched the dual images on the screens in the room: the cardiologist was calmly sharing the verdict of Bev's ultrasound while the TV announced that yet another giant metal bird had crashed.

Bev had a coarctation of the aorta and would need thoracic heart surgery. An active, lively baby who had started walking at nine months, she'd had only one sign of frailty, her always cold feet. Now we learned this was a result of poor blood circulation. Scheduling the surgery would take months of waiting anxiously for a date to circle on the calendar.

Roosting in my safe and controlled perch, I finished the mural until it shined. Its completion was celebrated while we still waited for a surgery date and prayed. Thankfully, Michael and I had a strong faith in common because now we would need it and the support of our flock more than ever.

My Friend Lucie

Sally Parsonson

C an you imagine having a Ferris wheel and merry-go-round in your backyard? You probably think that you would have to live within an amusement park to have such play equipment. But my friend Lucie with her little sister and two brothers lived in an ordinary 1930s brick house on Cedar Street in Greenville, Mississippi. In back of their house on its average-sized lot was an amusement park with not only a motorized Ferris wheel and merry-go-round but also a large metal jungle gym, tall wooden swings, a seesaw, a sandbox, and a swimming pool.

When I first saw this incredible layout, I was not as amazed as you might think. My family had just moved to Greenville. I was six years old. My mother had met Mrs. Robertson and determined that it was safe for me to go across the street alone to play. I don't remember that I ever wondered whether everyone, except for me, had this kind of play equipment in their backyard.

With the intense summer heat of the Mississippi Delta, my actual memories of playing with Lucie center more on indoor scenes with dolls or games. Lacking Toys 'R Us stores in those days, my father had built me a large dollhouse, which Lucie and I often enjoyed at my house. When we played in Lucie's bedroom on the second floor of her house, I remember climbing up the stairs as almost as much of a novelty for me as her backyard because I had never lived in a two-story house.

Outdoors at Lucie's house we played on the swings and seesaw or in the almost-always-dry-and-full-of-leaves swimming pool. The Ferris wheel and merry-go-round only worked on occasional Saturdays when Lucie's father was there to operate the motors. He had built everything himself for his four children and their friends. But he was also the repairman, and it usually took at least half a day for him to restore the equipment to working order. Meanwhile, all the children in the neighborhood had arrived, with everyone exclaiming, "When can we ride?" "Is it fixed yet?" "I get first turn." Often, even before we each got a turn, some part would break down. Mr. Robertson would announce: "Okay, this ride's closed." We returned to the child-powered swings and seesaw, scuffling our toes in the dust.

Later I learned that Mr. Robertson worked as an accountant, but why he built that play equipment is still a mystery. It was a unique place. But to me, aged six and new in town, the playground didn't have as much of a "wow" factor as it does in my memory. I suspect that whoever lives in the house now tore down the "Robertson Amusement Park," filled in the cracked swimming pool, and created a suburban lawn. But underneath the grass lie metal screws and slivers of wood along with memories of the lost park and my friendship with Lucie.

Deep Water

Christy Baker Knight

I n 2002 we were entering the deep water where faith, trust, and family float as lifesavers. Our one-year-old daughter would need heart surgery, and we had already waited six months for a date to be scheduled. Then, with a month's notice, we were told to bring her in to the children's hospital at dawn on a late June morning.

Meanwhile, my latest work as an artist was all about tidepools which I was preparing for a family show with my mother and sister at the Swan Coach House Gallery in Atlanta. These tiny worlds and the dreamy deeper water places beyond them had become an obsession.

The tidepools are aglow with light, pattern, and brilliant color. Nestled among the rocks along a jagged Maine coastline, these microcosms tell a story of life surviving protected from but connected to the massive ocean. Crustose Algae, Blue Mussel, Periwinkle, Rock Barnacle, Irish Moss, Ribbon Weed, and Knotted Wrack inhabit the gray rocks in the mid-littoral zone of this ecosystem. Compositions made up of these organisms change with every ebb and flow of the tides, and in a fleeting moment, tiny dramas unfold as low tide sends the pounding surf out to sea.

My Tidepools were painted in brilliant gouache watercolor on black paper, a medium I had used as a planetarium artist at Fernbank. On black, the fluid and opaque properties of gouache pop out just like tidepool life against dull gray rock. The natural forms of sea life lend themselves to the contrast of positive and negative space, and so this approach produced rich results.

We handed our baby girl over to the surgeon team, surrendering to the surreal wonder that humans can fix other humans. Granny and Paps came to visit, waiting and praying with us. They had lost a daughter at ten years of age, and old wounds surfaced as we paddled in a sea of uncertainty. Granny's eyes were glazed with Alzheimer's, but she rallied as they did what parents do, staying strong and helping us in every way they could. They fed pets and rotated shifts from the hospital to our home. Our whole community cushioned us like tender weeds, sheltering us from the waves of fear and pain, until a week later when Baby Bev came home. At her cardiology checkup, she slid down the high back of the crinkled paper chair. She was, and still is now at twenty years old, as resilient as the tidepools.

A month later, my extended family who live at the Jersey Shore visited for the art opening. Bev was healed, running around in her dress with the other children, giggling. As for Maine, at age six she got to spend a beautiful vacation week with us there. She lost her first tooth, built a volcano on the beach, hiked to the top of Mt. Desert Island, and walked on the rocks as I showed her the real tidepools.

THE ACCIDENT

Stefan Fatzinger

January 10, 1990 was to be a day of life, death, and miracles. The headline of the Rhein-Neckar Zeitung paper the following morning read, "A Nightmare That Became Reality" ("Alptraum Wurde Wahr"). But that fateful Wednesday began like any ordinary day.

It was a cold and damp German morning, typical for January, when the knock at the door announced the arrival of the new company employee, Bob Moore. My goal was to provide Bob with some on-the-job training for the next several days, the planned route taking us to Heilbronn, Ulm, Stuttgart, and Heidelberg. As he entered the house and saw me in just a suit and tie, he said, "It's damp and cold outside. You'd better wear a coat." I never liked to wear a coat in a car when I traveled because I found it too confining and restricting when bound by a seatbelt, but to humor him and not start our day on the wrong foot, I took off my suit jacket and put on my wool dress coat. As fate would have it, that decision would save my life.

We had left our first stop in Heilbronn and were on the A6 heading to the A7, the autobahn that leads to the city of Ulm, our next stop. There being no speed limits on the German autobahn, we were traveling at a very normal 160 kilometers, or 100 miles per hour, when we were suddenly engulfed by a thick fog near Braunsbach. We did not know it at the time, but we were on the highest bridge in Germany—the Kochertal Bruecke which stands 607 feet above the ground. Visibility was limited to where I could hardly see the hood of my car. I immediately took my foot off the accelerator and downshifted into a lower gear to begin slowing down. I had just accomplished this action when the forms of two trucks that were jackknifed across the highway with a car between them blocking all lanes appeared in the mist before me, leaving me no time even to hit the brakes. I simply took my foot off the accelerator and plowed into the melee at a speed between 60 and 70 miles per hour. This happened before cars had airbags, but the seatbelts worked as they grabbed me like a sumo wrestler and held my upper torso firmly in place.

After the collision, I turned to Bob in the passenger seat. He had a slightly bloodied nose from where his eyeglasses had caused a cut when he threw his hands in front of his eyes as he realized we were going to collide with the scene in front of us. Otherwise, he seemed unharmed. And then vehicles, as they entered the fog bank behind me, began slamming into my car from the rear, and I not only heard the sounds of metal on metal but felt jolt after jolt as my car was continuously pummeled by the oncoming traffic piling up behind me.

After the very first impact, Bob panicked and threw open the passenger door and jumped out. For the next minute or so I was hit approximately ten additional times by other vehicles as they too entered the fog bank and were met by a nightmare of cars strewn across the autobahn in front of them. I later discovered that 72 vehicles were involved, and ours was number 4 at the front of the pack. After being thumped, smashed, and rocked like a bumper car in an amusement park, the collisions stopped, and I was still alive. I also found myself unharmed, or so I thought. Recognizing that I appeared to be okay, I began looking around my car to get my bearings, worrying about what must have happened to Bob and thinking that he was dead, hit by one or more of the vehicles that had hit me after he leapt out of the car. I noticed that my car was now jammed between the two trucks, meaning that my car had pushed the other car further forward. I also was hearing a dripping sound like water from a faucet and looked around to discover where the sound might be coming from. I could no longer see out of the windshield; it was now a puzzle of crisscrossing lines, like glass hit with a hammer. But looking out the passenger window, I noticed drops coming out of the fuel tank of the truck to my right. As in a cartoon, those drops suddenly turned to flame and shot downwards and under the passenger door. Within seconds, the passenger seat, where Bob would have been had he not jumped out, was engulfed in flames. Then the fire raced to the backseat. Aided by the piles of paper that had just been stored there days before, after our beginning-of-year meeting, the whole backseat became an inferno. Fortunately, the forward middle console was serving as a firebreak protecting the driver seat from catching fire. But I was surrounded by fire. Terrified I said to myself, "Self, we need to get of here!"

My first thought was to kick out the shattered piece of glass that had been the windshield. But two things occurred when I attempted this maneuver. The first was that, although shattered, the glass would not give and break. The second was that when I bent backward to lift my leg to assist me in breaking the glass, the hair on my head disappeared, being singed by the flames in the backseat, leaving only little black balls where my hair had been only moments before. I was left with one alternative: I had to escape through the driver's door but being jammed up against a truck only allowed the door to open approximately 6 inches, not wide enough for my body, or any body for that matter, not even that of a child. But with fire to the right of me and behind me, I was left with no alternative. And then time stopped for me, and what I am about to relate I can only see in my mind as still pictures like those found in a photo album, rather than one continuous film as in a movie or video. I was also aware once again of that Presence that had visited me when I was twelve.

My first memory is battling to undo my seatbelt because the center console was bent over the catch release. After successfully unbinding myself from the seatbelt, I was next able to force my head through the small opening in the top of the driver's door. But then my shoulders became stuck. However, through sheer terror, I was able to force those stubborn shoulders through the top of the door, only to discover that my chest was now the stumbling block. Pushing upwards with the extra strength that fear, adrenaline, and perhaps God were providing, my chest bent the doorframe, and I broke free before I once again became thwarted by the belt that bound my wool coat. Fortunately, wool doesn't burn which is why I am able today to tell my tale; that wool coat, which still hangs in my closet, saved my life. But at the time that coat was also my challenge. With my upper torso above the car door frame, I began pushing down on the top of the door with all my remaining strength. Suddenly the belt buckle exploded, releasing the belt, allowing me to pull the lower half of my body through the top of the door. As I pulled my legs out of the car, I stretched and slid onto the truck's fuel tank that had been blocking my ability to open my car door. Within the split second that I stood up on the fuel tank, my car exploded, propelling me through the air like a ball shot from a cannon for about twenty feet. I landed on the hood of the car that I had originally rammed when all this began. No sooner had I reached the car hood than the fuel tank I had been standing on exploded! The concussion of the explosion knocked me off the car and onto the autobahn. I stood shaking my head, thankful to be alive. Smoke was billowing off the back of my coat, and I began striking and beating the coat thinking I was on fire, forgetting for the moment that wool does not burn. And then I looked at the scene behind me. Cars were burning, people were screaming, and a wall of flame two to three stories high covered the entire eastbound A6. I later learned that twenty people were injured and that six died in the carnage that I was now witnessing. Five victims were consumed by the fire that was burning unabated.

My thoughts now turned exclusively to Bob who, if alive, was on the other side of the flames. I had to find him, but the wall of fire prevented me from getting to where I thought Bob must be. After about thirty minutes, fire trucks and ambulances began arriving across the median on the westbound lanes of the A6. A lone fireman walked across the median and sprayed some sort of chemical on the asphalt that put out the fire for about five feet, creating a door in the flames. Without hesitation or thought, I walked through that door to the other side of the flames and began looking for Bob. After about five minutes of searching, I heard a voice: "Stefan?" I turned in the direction of the voice and spotted Bob sitting on the side of the highway. His nose was bloody, and he was missing a shoe that he lost when he leapt out of the car. The sight of the two of us must have been comical—him with the bloody nose and missing a shoe and me with singed hair. But we didn't notice. We were both ecstatic at having thought each other dead and discovering that we were both alive. He stood up and hugged me. I would have hugged him back, but his hug sent a searing pain through my chest, and I gasped in agony, the first pain I had felt since the accident began. He released me with concern and asked, "Are you all right?" "No," was my answer. "I have an excruciating pain in my chest." Concerned, Bob found a doctor, and, with great German efficiency, we were both loaded into an ambulance and were soon on our way to the hospital.

At the hospital it was discovered that I probably had several broken ribs, presumably caused by my seatbelt, but possibly by the car door as I forced my way through. Except for minor scratches, Bob was found to be just fine, but the doctors wanted to run some further tests on my chest. With other victims in worse condition than we were, my medical team went off to examine them. As soon as the examining room was empty, I got up, found Bob, and said, "Let's go!" He looked at me incredulously but didn't argue. We walked out the hospital's front door, and I hailed a cab, instructing the driver to take me home, a 120-mile journey. While we were in the taxi on our trip back to Sinsheim, the police had called my wife to explain that I had been in a terrible accident, was taken to the hospital, but had disappeared! So, you can imagine her reaction when Bob and I walked in the house, he with one shoe and a bloody nose, and I with singed hair and sore ribs. She turned pale and fell to the floor.

That night a liter of Jack Daniels disappeared, and the nightmares began. The next morning, I visited my family doctor across the street. He taped my ribs and provided me with pain medication. But it was soul medication that I really needed. It would be weeks before I was able to close my eyes and not have the accident replayed over again in my mind. I could not even get behind the wheel of a car. To this day I can still hear the screams of the people that were not as fortunate as I was and who had remained trapped in their cars while they were consumed by fire. But time does heal, not just the body, but also the mind.

And my car? Curiosity got the better of me and a week after the accident, I had my wife drive me to the lot where it had been towed. The hunk of metal that I saw was no longer recognizable as an automobile. Everything that could have burned—rubber, plastic, upholstery, glass—no longer existed. And the metal shell that remained was not only still smoldering but looked like a metal can that had been trampled by a herd of elephants. Perhaps the best description was provided by the gentleman behind the desk at the lot. When I arrived, I requested to see the car. He asked me who I was, and when I responded that I was the driver, he refused to believe me. He just shook his head and said, "*Unmoeglich*," which in German means *impossible*. He next added, "The driver of that car is no longer alive!" But, of course, I was and am still alive. "Why, you ask?" I have given that question much thought over the ensuing years. The only reasonable answer that I have been able to manufacture is found in the words that end every Episcopal service: "Thanks be to God!"

Coming Back from the Ledge

Jeannie Longley

O n a recent trip to New England, my husband and I had the chance to stay with a friend in the coastal town of Rockport, Massachusetts. We had never been there and found it to be a charming area. At one time it was home to many granite quarries as well as boatyards and a large fishing industry. The cottage we stayed in was built on the edge of a hill and was reportedly at one time a storage area for feed for the oxen that pulled the wagons of granite. The interior wall was made of roughly-hewn granite, which was not only rustic, but kept the rooms cool.

The first morning after we arrived was a crisp clear day with temperatures in the low 60s at sunrise. I went for a refreshing run along the coastline. My friend and I were joined by another friend of hers, and we all headed to an old quarry for a morning swim.

The quarry was typical of many in the area: it was no longer active and went down to a depth of a few hundred feet. Over the years, it had filled with rainwater and made a grand swimming area. There were a couple of other folks swimming, but otherwise it was deserted. The water was warmer than the air at that time of day but was still refreshing. After scraping my knee on the ledge of cut rock, I decided to follow the others out toward the middle of the quarry.

Although I can swim, it has never been my strong suit, in part because I never liked the chlorine in most swimming pools. And though I can run for a long time without getting tired, one lap of the crawl will render me breathless and make my heart pound. So most of the time I do the breaststroke or sidestroke.

I hadn't really paid attention to how far out we swam, but when I looked back, I realized that it was a long way back to the shore. I headed back, trying to stay calm, but I began to panic. I said nothing to my friend because I didn't want to alarm her, and I certainly didn't want to make her panic. I recalled stories of swimmers who had pulled others down while flailing about in the water. I started thinking about how deep the water was, how far it was to the shore, how few people were there, and the lack of any lifeguard or life-saving equipment. At some point I realized that I just needed to get hold of myself and not let my fear amplify my situation. I stopped for a moment just to tread water. I took a mental inventory of how I was feeling: breathing was not too labored, legs were working fine, and I was staying afloat. I told myself there was no reason for alarm, but I still had a long way to go.

Back at the edge, the other people who were swimming had taken an incredibly long log, which was floating by the shore, and had rotated it out into the quarry so that they could jump off of it. I set my sights on that log and made a beeline for it. After what seemed like an eternity but was in fact probably just a few minutes, I reached that log. My heart was racing, and my breathing rapid. But in just a short while, I was fine. I knew on one level that the danger had been mainly in my head, but I also realized how that sort of thinking can take over and lead to disaster. The next time I swim in a quarry I may just stay closer to the edge.

CANOEING IN MAINE

Tony Clarke

I n New England when you say the river name, the Allagash, canoeists' eyes light up and visions appear of that iconic Maine river running north through forested countryside up to Canada. A canoer's delight, the river abounds with rapids and turbulent waters and miles and miles of great scenery. Now designated an official wilderness area, the Allagash River is one of the most traveled rivers in a very isolated area of the sparsely populated northern portion of Maine, where logging, fishing, and hunting are the main industries.

Having traveled to Maine on several occasions for business or pleasure while living in Hingham, Massachusetts, I was always fascinated by the beauty of Maine's forested countryside and its idyllic remoteness. In 1969, to attract the urban dwellers in Boston, Maine filled many billboards in that area with its inviting advertisement "Ahhhhhh Maine." I was hooked with getting into Maine and paddling on its pristine rivers and lakes. My son Bill, our oldest child, was in the Boy Scouts so a trip there could be a wonderful adventure and education for him.

Although I didn't pretend to be an expert outdoorsman, I felt comfortable that with my previous camping experiences and three years of Army service, including over one year in the field, we'd do well. And while we didn't have cell phones or any connections in the woods and on the lake, we felt we would be all right. So I thought, "Let's do it," and with no real objections from my wife, we put the operation in motion. I wouldn't think of doing this now, but the spirit of adventure and excitement was overwhelming.

On the topographical maps we laid out our itinerary for this week-long excursion in which we would spend two days driving and six days on the water. Our plan was to drive over to the southeast corner of Lake Telos and put in there after staying that night. We'd paddle that lake the first day and get to Lake Chamberlain the second day, then head up the Little Allagash River and by the third day reach Lake Allagash, and then turn around and retrace our steps back to the starting point and our car.

We packed as lightly as we could, but with a six-day supply of food, rain gear, tent, fishing poles, life jackets, and our clothes, plus miscellaneous stuff, we had a load. We were eager so off we went with our 17-foot metal Grumman canoe strapped to the top of the car.

After seven and half hours of driving we reached our launching spot on Lake Telos. Arriving in daylight with the sun out, the expanse of the lake couldn't have been more beautiful. We were thrilled and got busy setting up our tent and fixing our first night's freeze-dried meal. At this point I should mention we didn't carry any water except for canteens we filled up with lake water, which we were told on good authority was safe to drink. Would I drink untreated lake water now? Not likely. But these were remote lakes, and since they were in boundary water off the Allagash River System where no motors of any kind were allowed in the area and campers carried out what they carried in, and with not many people traveling or canoeing these areas, we felt it was safe. It's far different today as everyone has discovered these previously untouched areas then owned primarily by timber companies and conservancies.

For the most part the excursion went as planned, with some exceptions. In the process we learned in a few days much about canoeing and the back country of Maine. We learned that the rain in Maine falls mainly in the plain and everywhere else in abundance. We spent the major part of the second day on a small island in Lake Chamberlain huddled in our little tent trying to stay both dry and warm. Something else we discovered was if people get wet in Maine, and the sun isn't out, they are going to be very chilled, so they either hunker down or paddle like mad. We also found moving our canoe on a windswept lake was very hard work. In fact, in trying to cross the center of one lake against the wind and one-foot waves we had to go around the protected shoreline of the lake tacking like a sailboat against the wind.

The scenery on the lakes was beautiful, and there was always a wall of trees surrounding the shore. Around many of the lakes were considerable areas of bogs which were impossible to camp in since there was no high ground. We had to search diligently along the shoreline for the few marked campsites maintained by the park service. These could be hard to find if one were searching any distance from the shore.

One of the interesting places we discovered between Lake Chamberlain and Eagle Lake was a home maintained by the lockkeeper and his wife. I recall they said they lived there the best part of the year in total isolation except for a long-distance radio and the radio telephone they used for connection with park headquarters. We bought their delightful little book, *Away From It All*, about their experiences over 30 years of lock keeping and how they maintained themselves and the lock over that period.

Our only disappointment was that we couldn't get up the Little Allagash River from Lake Chamberlain to Lake Allagash. As hard as we tried with paddle, pole, and portage, the river, really just a creek, was too small and steep to navigate upstream. Coming back down we had our only close encounter with capsizing when we got turned around on a rock ledge. We got the canoe straightened out after a bit and maneuvered downstream safely to the lake.

Our biggest adventure, outside of paddling, sight-seeing, and catching a small fish or two, was crossing back over Chamberlain on our last night. Around dusk, heading for the campsite across the lake, we ran into a lightning storm and immediately got off the lake. Standing in a boggy area as darkness approached, we could see a camp light across the lake and realized eventually it would be turned off and we would have difficulty locating that camp in the woods. We couldn't stay all night in the bog, and we were wet and hungry. After some hesitation I finally decided, "Let's go for it." I realized we were the perfect target on the open lake for a random bolt of lightning. Off we went and were three-fourths of the way across when suddenly we stopped. I shouted at my son in the front of the boat, "Paddle harder," and he replied, "I'm going as hard as I can." In our excitement, it took me a minute to realize our front mooring line had caught on an underwater tree branch. We had to cut the line to clear it. Heading to shore, we were greeted by a young couple who had spotted us earlier and not only put on the lantern that we saw but saved us some of their spaghetti dinner and a nip of bourbon which we enjoyed thoroughly. Then very quickly after being with our new friends, we set up our tent, in the rain of course, got rid of our wet clothes, and proceeded to fall into a long deep sleep.

I've misplaced the pictures, but I still have the lockkeeper's book which is a wonderful reminder of this great adventure. My son was an excellent camper and good paddler even when I thought he was slacking off as we raced across the lake in that lightning storm. He enjoyed the canoe trip as much as I did and has plans for an odyssey on the Chattahoochee when time permits. As for me, I am still paddling in my dreams.

THE LETTER IN THE INSIDE POCKET

Janet Wilson

The vacant lot sits at the crest of the hill just to the right of the old trestle bridge. Once a year we would drive across that bridge to Croton Point Park where we would join other families of railroad men for a picnic. Seeing that vacant lot leaves me feeling empty and alone.

Though I have no recollection of my first train ride, I have many memories of riding the train with Grandpa. He often came up to see us, and he would bring our favorite treats—Hershey bars, Jewish marble pound cake, and a heavenly chocolate cream pie. Sometimes I went back to the Bronx with him. Mom and Dad took us to Croton-Harmon station where we all walked down the long, steep stairway taking us from the building that once stood on the lot to the tracks below. If Grandma were with us, she rode the freight elevator instead. Grandma was all of five feet tall, round-bodied, and in need of exercise. But she pouted if she had to climb up or down stairways needlessly.

Grandpa always reminded my sisters and me to stand behind the yellow line on the platform as we waited for our train. There we watched and waited. Then almost in unison the three of us would cover our ears. We giggled and shouted trying to be heard over the screams of arrivals and departures. It was here, at this place, that Grandpa delivered me home to Mom and Dad and my two sisters, shortening my ten-day summer vacation to four.

The phone rang five times before Grandma got to it. It was shortly before dinnertime. I remember Grandma had been busy in the kitchen since returning home from our outing which included shopping at Alexander's, a movie at the Loew's Paradise Theater, and ice cream at Krums—a chocolate sundae for me and a banana split topped with pineapple for Grandma. (She loved pineapple.) It was the same day Grandma had had an argument with not one, but two of the salesgirls at Alexander's. She was entitled to an extra gift box, and she was not going to leave without one.

We had been sitting at the kitchen table where Grandma was teaching me how to make paper boats using ordinary paper napkins and pieces of New York Central stationery. Some minutes passed when Grandma rejoined me at the kitchen table with our growing fleet of paper vessels. Something was different about Grandma. She reached into her apron pocket and handing me a fistful of change asked me to run to the grocer's for a bottle of milk. Then, turning quickly, she faced the sink and attended to the contents within. I wanted to say "Is everything okay?" but I didn't. This seemed like one of those times when Grandma needed to be alone. I unlatched the chain and the double lock on the door and headed downstairs to the grocery store just around the corner. No one was in the courtyard outside the building's entrance. I guess they had all gone in to eat...even the grumpy old lady in the end apartment on the ground floor who spent most of her time at one or the other of her windows yelling at children to go away. She was so bothered by noisy children that she filled pots with water and then threw the water out her windows to drench them.

"Hi, Mr. Mandel," I said. He smiled and answered, "Well, how are you this evening? So we're doing a little shopping for Grandma, eh?"

"I'm fine, thank you." I always said that I was fine, though at times I wasn't. "I'll only need this for tonight," I said, handing him the milk bottle.

Returning up five flights of stairs to Grandma and Grandpa's at 2363 Valentine Avenue, I entered the apartment and latched the chain. A sudden chill of fear stopped me from continuing toward the kitchen, the long hallway seeming longer than I ever knew it to be. Did Grandma really need milk? I wondered.

Placing the bottle of milk into the refrigerator, or icebox as Grandma would say, I saw that milk had not been needed. Grandma was sitting in her favorite place next to the kitchen window where she loved to watch passersby...and sometimes mischievously shook her dustmop over their heads. Her cheeks were wet; her eyes filled with sadness.

"What's the matter, Grandma?"

"The phone call earlier was from Grandpa's sister, Aunt Edythe in Canada," she answered trying not to cry. A phone call from Revelstoke...I was afraid of what Grandma was about to tell me.

"Great Grandpa has been rushed to the hospital. The doctors don't yet know what is wrong, but your great-grandpa is seriously ill." Grandpa would be home any time now. Every evening he takes the train from his office at the Yonkers Freight Yard to University Heights. Grandpa loves to walk, so from there he walks home. After a brief hello he likes to take a twenty-minute nap before sitting down to dinner and conversation. Tonight we would have to tell him about Aunt Edythe's call.

My grandpa is a family man. He loves family gatherings for Thanksgiving, Christmas, and Easter. He loves family birthday celebrations. Grandpa wishes his two daughters and sons-in-law, six grandchildren, and eleven great-grandchildren would gather together more often.

My grandpa cries. When he is sad, he cries sad tears. When he is worried, he cries worried tears. Sometimes he cries sad, worried tears. Grandpa even cries happy tears. Sometimes when I see Grandpa's tears, I begin to tear up myself.

Grandpa was born in Italy. During rescue efforts following a major earthquake in a little town not far from Calabria, he was found safely cradled in his mother's arms in the doorway of a collapsed building where she died. Not long after, my great-grandfather left Italy, settling his family in Revelstoke, British Columbia. Grandpa's boyhood was spent there. He was at home in this simple railroad town nestled in the grandeur of the Canadian Rockies. At nineteen, though, he and a close friend, Domenic Critelli, sneaked across the Canadian border and made their way to the big city, New York, where both found jobs with the New York Central Railroad. I have always felt that Grandpa was torn between two worlds...two families. I think his heart remains suspended over the Canadian-U.S. border. Whenever he receives a letter from Canada, he cries happy-sad tears, and I am reminded of his deep love for his other home and the people he misses. Sometimes he reads the letters to me, but mostly he keeps them as secret treasures.

It was an unusually quiet dinnertime that night. After dinner, Grandpa dialed the long-distance number, then talked to Aunt Edythe, jotting down bits of information as they spoke. Later, we three sat together in the quiet of the living room. The familiar chimes of Grandma's clock resting on top of the television sounded in the silence. Grandpa, all choked up, explained his plans. He would leave with me in the morning. We would ride together to Croton-Harmon station. Mom, Dad, and my sisters would meet us there. I knew the rest... we'd all give Grandpa kisses and hugs and our prayers, sending him on alone. Oh, how I wished I could go with him! Over the next three days and two nights on the train he would journey nearly 3,000 miles with no one beside him...with no one to understand his pain, with too much time to fear what he would learn on his arrival in Revelstoke. I don't know how I slept that night. I wonder if Grandpa slept at all.

It wasn't until after we boarded the train, Grandpa and I, that I was struck by an urgency to write a letter. I recalled the story my sister, Diane, told from time to time. She was lucky. She had met our great-grandparents. In September of the year I first entered school, my grandparents had taken Diane with them to Canada. I'd always felt a little angry about that, though I suppose I shouldn't. Why did they go to Revelstoke when I wasn't able to go?

I held back the tears and tried not to think about the picture I had in mind...the one of Great Grandpa pretending to be a monster. Moving slowly, with arms curved and held forward, his fingers arched and pointed, he would grumble deep, dark frightening sounds. My sister remembers the sounds and the look of this pretend monster. I looked up at Grandpa and asked for a piece of paper. He always had one of his New York Central Railroad pads with him.

I wrote to my great-grandpa. I don't remember the words I used. I do remember the love with which they were written. And I remember feeling better after having written them. I reread my message, then lovingly sealed it in its envelope. Handing it to Grandpa, I said, "Please take this to Great Grandpa. I want him to know I am thinking about him and I love him. Tell him to get well quickly. And tell him I hope to meet him soon."

Grandpa tucked the envelope safely into the inside pocket of his overcoat as we pulled into Croton-Harmon station.

All these years have passed and only now, as I look at this empty lot, am I suddenly haunted by that time...by that letter. Grandpa is dying. He has cancer. I never did find the right time to ask him if my letter reached my great-grandpa. I never did meet Great Grandpa.

Dolores

Beverly Baker

I'm looking at a photo of my Aunt Dolores and me at the Jersey Shore. She looks casual, yet alert and highly confident. Her pose shows off her tall girlish figure and good-looking legs. She is smiling, her gaze fixed on the photographer. Her bathing suit is white with colorful polka dots. I remember it clearly to this day. It was a typical one-piece suit as worn in the mid-nineteen-forties.

In the photo, I am sitting near her scrunched up in a hole I had just dug out. We look as though we are happy to have our picture taken, and we were. We were buddies. Aunt Dolores was my grown-up friend. She loved being with me, and I adored following her around. She was in her twenties then, and I was around six.

Aunt Dolores was studying to be a medical photographer. She took her future career very seriously and always had her camera, a twin-lens reflex, with her.

She'd suddenly say, "Practice makes perfect," and zoom off to take a picture.

At the beach, she took pictures of the sea and fishermen putting out from shore in the long dory boats of the day. When I look at these pictures now, they seem to be period pieces, romantic sepia images of men and boats plying their craft. The pictures are classically composed and steeped in nostalgia. But that is one of photography's tricks. It documents a time and place even though that may not be the photographer's intention.

The dory men were young and muscular. If one were to put Aunt Dolores's pictures in Photoshop, say, color them up and superimpose modern techno-gear on the figures, they would look like today's sea-faring guys fooling around with antique boats. But those doctored-up pictures would be fictitious.

I think that Aunt Dolores wanted to take clear, sharp, and accurate pictures of what fascinated her at the seaside and also in New York City. I don't think that she wanted to make self-conscious artistic statements. She was more of a scientist as her future work at the hospital would reveal. And she was always up for a challenge.

During the war, she got a job at the Bendix Corporation—job title: "Rosey the Riveter." The war changed everything, and, afterwards there was a collective momentum, a kind of frenzy to go for the

American Dream. To be upwardly mobile was the prime directive. The modern age had arrived.

Plastics and polyester were enveloping us like an alien ooze. It was a new pop imprint on all things great and small which would change our visual landscape forever. Garish colors, bulbous shapes, sprouted everywhere especially in the toy world. The traditional exquisitely hand-painted porcelain dolls gave way to plastic renditions of the cute popular cartoon stars. Disney ruled. The first time I fell in love was with Bambi on the big screen.

At the beach, I carried Aunt Dolores's camera bag while she went about her work. I tried to keep it dry and safe with the good intentions of a six-year-old. But I remember now that there was one wave—oops! Oh, no! I scrambled desperately to rescue the camera kit from the smashing surf. Luckily, it was zipped and fairly-waterproof. She took it in stride, being more interested in taking her pictures than in scolding me.

There were twelve square negatives on her 120 black-and-white film. She had to get it right the first time. I sometimes wonder what she would think about today's haphazard digital excess—take a hundred rapid-fire shots, certainly there will be one or two keepers at the least. I don't think she'd like the digital world. She was way too careful and methodical. Even when she moved to 35-mm color slide film, she maintained the same dedication to lighting, subject, and compositional perfection.

When I was a couple of years older, she gave me a Kodak Brownie for Christmas. I still have it carefully stored away in my camera collection along with her old Rollie which her brother gave me after she died. Old cameras have a special smell that conjures up memories.

A few years later, when I was considering a career in art and had developed a serious interest in photography, she invited me to her lab at the Cornell Medical School hospital in New York City. I was both thrilled and horrified by the experience. She was in the process of documenting wretched skin conditions on malformed patients. They were more like creatures than people. Years later, I recognized this condition in the movie, *The Elephant Man*. While there, leafing through her photos, I began to think about how my beautiful, generous, and spirited aunt had been surrounded by images of profound suffering on a daily basis for years. I realized that there was something saintly about her photographic encounters. Even her given name of Spanish origin translates as "Our Lady of Sorrow: a title of the Virgin Mary," which seems to have foreshadowed her life's calling.

Many years later, when the art world developed a taste for shock value, my aunt's documents of pain were the real thing—nothing contrived. She is still teaching me. I miss her.

As an afterthought, I must add that she was not my biological aunt but my mother's best childhood friend. She never married and lived with her father most of her life. Her mother had died early on while giving birth to a stillborn child.

PART THREE

My Path to Korea

Tony Clarke

In June of 1950 I had returned home on summer vacation from my sophomore year in college with no money or job prospects providing some money for my junior year. In my small town of Columbia, Kentucky (population 2500), there were few jobs to be had except temporary farm work on the burley tobacco farms, to which I had no reliable transportation. My parents had things I could do for them, but nothing that could bring in any funds to my need on hand, so I had a problem.

My buddy Charley Antle, also home from college, proposed a partial solution to resolve this situation. He asked me, "How would you like a job that would pay you $25 for a couple of hours once a week and also meet some nice guys?" When I asked for details, he told me, "We go over to Campbellsville, Kentucky, 25 miles away, and join their unit of the Kentucky National Guard. They will pay us each $25 for every weekly meeting we attend." I was impressed and came to the conclusion it was a great idea.

The great idea was put into motion on the next drill date of the Campbellsville unit of the Kentucky National Guard, Battery B of the 623rd Field Artillery Battalion. The headquarters battery of the battalion was located in Glasgow, and the Service Battery, Battery A, and Battery C in other small Kentucky towns. Battery B was approximately at 50% of full strength, so Charley's and my enlistments were warmly welcomed.

But a strange thing happened that caught us by surprise. We had enlisted on June 20th in 1950 and then on June 25th North Korea invaded South Korea. The net effect was that our enlistments were frozen. Up to June 25th, if you wanted to back out of your enlistment, you could. But after June 25th all enlistments were frozen, and you could not get out. Charley and I, or at least I, had not been following world events too closely, but I was not concerned that we could eventually be in harm's way. That attitude was to change, however, as weeks went by and North Korea was overwhelming South Korea.

Monday drills in Campbellsville were interesting and usually enjoyable. There were lectures by the officers on military protocol, our weapons, tractor-drawn 155 mm howitzers, other battery equipment and vehicles, organizational structures, individual duties, all the things we needed to know to operate efficiently. Since our weapons were in storage at Ft. Knox, we had no access to them. But being confined to our armory we could do close-order drill, and lots of it, to shape us into some semblance of a military unit. It took a while for me to enjoy it, but anybody who had half of an appearance of leadership was required to be in charge of our marches up and down the armory floor. So I caught on quickly.

Soon it was August and the two-week National Guard training camp was being held at Ft. Knox. It was a busy time for live fire of our weapons, including support of infantry units, setting up telephone and radio communications, map reading, surveying of battery positions, fire-direction practice, transportation coordination, and a host of other details.

Persistent rumors ran through the camp about the future deployment of the battalion in the wake of South Korean losses in the war. We were all interested as to whether our unit might possibly be deployed abroad. One day, at a good time, I was able to ask our battery commander, Captain Oren Billingsley, "Captain, there's a persistent rumor going around camp that our battalion is going to be given rifles, two-weeks training with our guns, and sent over to Korea to help stem the tide in the war." Capt. Billingsley looked at me and said, "Son, if I'm not mistaken, you are in college so you won't be taken. I don't think you have any reason to be concerned."

Much relieved, I returned to school that fall of 1950 and entered my junior year putting aside any personal concern about going off to the Korean War. School went well. My major concern was whether I really wanted to stay on a pre-med direction. To that end I did take a one-semester course in College Algebra and Trigonometry as a pre-requisite for Calculus, a pre-requisite for medical school.

Just before our Christmas break classes ended and we entered the Reading Period, a three-week break to prepare for final exams and write papers due for our course grades. I headed home to Columbia for Christmas with family, and to complete my schoolwork.

Christmas Eve I was at home when I heard a knock on the door. When I answered, I was surprised to see Eugene Miller, our Battery B supply sergeant from Campbellsville. I said to him, "Hi, Gene. It's good to see you. What brings you here to Columbia on Christmas Eve?" He replied, "Well, I've got news for you. The Army has activated our unit, effective January 14th. All personnel will report that date for drill and to get further orders. We will leave for Ft. Bragg, North Carolina, soon after at a date to be determined for training." I then replied, "Well, I'll miss seeing you and the guys since I'll be returning to school."

Gene said, "You don't understand. You are going, too. They are taking everybody in the unit." I replied, "But I was told they wouldn't call up the guys that were in school." Gene commented, "Apparently that's not the case so I'll see you on the 14th. Merry Christmas." After he left I sat down to figure out if I should challenge the government on my status. It didn't take long for me to figure out that I wouldn't stand a chance disputing this, so the next question was how to get credit for three and a half months of coursework at school.

My professors at school were very sympathetic to my situation. One had me write a brief paper. Two others averaged my grades for the semester. One gave me an early test. In all cases I had passing grades for full credit.

On January 14, 1951, I reported for duty in Campbellsville ready for whatever was to follow. What followed was one of the most significant experiences in my life: the opportunity to serve my country for three years in the U.S. Army, which included one year (1952) in Korea with Battery B of the 623rd Field Artillery Battalion. As I look back on it, I realize how fortunate I was to be able to serve in spite of the danger, and to come out of it unharmed, a little smarter, more grounded, and very grateful. Truly I was fortunate, and to this day I value the experience as one of the most important of my life.

A BLOCK AT BLACK GAP

Christy Baker Knight

One reason people choose to attend Colorado College (otherwise known as CC) is for the intensive format called the Block Plan. There is no cramming for exams on different subjects all in the same week, something most high school graduates have had enough of all ready. Instead, students study one subject per month at a feverish pace, take one exam, and then go on a block break—a long weekend—to explore the breathtaking landscape. Yes, CC exists.

I had many amazing blocks and block breaks. My first month as a freshman involved reading, discussing, and writing about iconic American writers such as Sherwood Anderson and William Faulkner, and then backpacking through the New Mexico wilderness. Fallen aspen leaves glowed on our path in the twilight, lighting the way as we hiked to camp on an open mesa. When we were later rained and snowed upon, our group's sense of humor persevered as friendships formed.

Some blocks were harder or more tedious while others were gloriously inspired, but the most memorable class in my four years was the February into March I spent in the middle of the Chihuahuan Desert near Big Bend National Park. A dozen art students, a professor, and an assistant packed enough gear in a van to prepare to live in tents and draw the landscape of the Black Gap wilderness on the U.S.-Mexico Border.

We followed the Rio Grande (both river and train) south with a Valentine sunset sendoff through rolling New Mexico plains. After a second day's journey into the bowl-like landscape of west Texas, we finally spied rugged monoliths flanked by open mesas. Desert succulents—sharp yucca, agave, and cacti—warned us to watch our step. Below in the papery river cane on the banks of the Rio Grande we chose our tent rooms, the dry stalks offering privacy under an otherwise vast horizon. Beyond our nurturing home in the cane, the river meandered lazily, always a milky shade of brown with green shadows.

Our base camp was a roofless adobe relic, and we reclaimed this frontier outpost by holding classes and meals inside warmed by raging bonfires. Its rectangular windows framed the landscape, inspiring compositions. We began each day with some small direction by our fearless leader, Bogdan Swider, a short, bald, animated professor who acted ageless. Bogdan could draw with perfection and expected the same from us. He would scare us with a mistake-laden story from "the last class who came here" and then send us into the vast wilderness to find our vantage points. The sweet smell of skunk spray permeated our camp, and coyotes called in the surrounding desert. While we drew, some students were visited by a wandering javelina (wild boar), and the reenactment of their encounters with the tusked beast's approach had us buckling with laughter.

As an aspiring artist and naturalist, my icon was Georgia O'Keeffe, whose footsteps I followed in the desert. I chose a different landscape to draw each week, from the high monoliths to the endless mesa and then deep in the river cane along the water. Each afternoon we would regroup at base camp for critiques as we propped our drawing boards along the adobe wall. The breeze teased the heavy rag paper we had labored over for hours with graphite and charcoal lines and threatened to send our work sailing into the cerulean sky.

With no cell phones in 1989, our closest connection to civilization was the ranger station several miles away. We bathed in the soft river water with catfish rubbing our ankles and got fresh water from a spring nine miles up the road. One day it was cold enough for snow flurries, and we took a trip into town to stay warm. On a hotter day, our journey to the Mexican border town of Boquillas involved a harrowing river crossing in a tiny tin boat. Safely back at camp that night, we soaked in the stars over our fire circle.

We were truly in nature.

Four years later, I was able to recreate a diorama of Black Gap while working as an exhibit designer at Fernbank Museum of Natural History in Atlanta. I returned to Big Bend heading up a team of vivacious characters that included artist and naturalist extraordinaire—my mentor and lifelong friend, Mozelle Funderburk—along with a jolly taxidermist and a spunky carpenter, to research, document, and collect. This time we stayed near the ranger station in a fully equipped bunk house complete with a land line, but late at night I took my sleeping bag to the porch to be out in the desert once again and wake to the yip of coyotes in the sunrise over Black Gap.

I recently learned that a fellow CC student who had been on this journey with us, Seth Bossung, died in an avalanche while back-country skiing this winter. It seems appropriate to dedicate this memoir to him and his legacy as a celebrated Colorado resident and architect. I remember Seth as a bright spark, always up for adventures and conversations, with a passion for art, nature, and community—quite possibly the ultimate CC student.

When the Flying Fishes Played

Tony Clarke

When I was talking to my daughter Beth who mentioned looking for good seafood restaurants, flying fishes flew into the conversation. I thought immediately of flying fish when I was crossing the Pacific in 1951 en route to South Korea. Many days of this epic trip, I would see schools of flying fish racing our ship. Toward dusk the last rays of sunshine turned their sleek bodies into shimmering silver orange missiles reaching out to pass our ship. They were beautiful to watch. It brought a smile to everyone watching their magnificent glides and entry in and out of the water, a welcome change from the tedium of the days.

Our troop ship was on a voyage to carry our Kentucky National Guard unit, the 623rd Field Artillery Battalion, headquartered in Glasgow, Kentucky, to Korea, where heavy fighting was going on, to save South Korea from North Korea's invasion. My position was as a sergeant in Battery B, a firing battery, composed of 155mm howitzers. Had I not inadvertently joined the National Guard on June 20, 1950, I would have been a junior in college. This voyage was an eye- and mind-opening experience for me in which flying fish were a part of the scene.

In December 1951 our unit had been ordered to Korea to arrive later that month. We would start by train, men and equipment, from Ft. Bragg, North Carolina, to arrive in San Francisco, where we would board a troop ship to Yokohama, Japan, and then another smaller ship to Pusan, Korea, and its southern harbor. Our train to San Francisco took many days, and I took many pictures with my new Argus C3, my first camera dedicated to more serious photography.

The train ride was, in spite of its length, a fascinating trip between playing cards, talking, sightseeing, dozing, picture-taking, reading, and speculating about what lay ahead. At many places along the way where the train loaded up with coal or water, or to allow other trains to pass, we would "fall out" at the station and do calisthenics to keep us fit, physically and mentally. Our most memorable stop was Harvey, Arizona, when we detrained and were greeted by the local Harvey organization employees. We were, however, restricted to calisthenics for our stop. Beautiful southwest scenery was outstanding, especially Texas, New Mexico, and Arizona. Two pictures I particularly treasured were of sandstone buttes in Texas, or Arizona, and the mountains in southern California. My favorite indoor shot was down the length of the rail car. Two cook assistants are lugging a kettle of soup up the aisle dishing it out into paper bowls to the GIs in their seats.

At last we arrived in San Francisco. We were to stay on the train overnight with the understanding we would detrain the next morning, take buses to the dock, and board our troop ship. However, my friend, Charlie Antle, and I took off for a brief look at San Francisco, but we didn't see much, not having a travel guide or the time, as we had been ordered to be back at an early hour. One in our group had told us about a famous nightclub, Bimbo's 365 Club, with food, which sounded good to us, and a naked lady in an aquarium, even better.

Charlie and I set off for this bonanza, found it, and were seated at the table. I was eager to see the spectacle in the aquarium, so I left Charlie to order meals for us. When I got to the aquarium in the lobby, I found that it was a large aquarium, but too small to accommodate a person. As I was looking this over, the maître d' told me, "Go check out the viewing window in the rock in the seaweed." I did and was rewarded with a view of a stark-naked woman lying on a covered table doing what would be termed a table dance. She was visible on the floor below through a device like a reverse periscope built into the rock.

I was astounded almost as much by the engineering of this phenomenon, as by this lovely, young lady of amazing stature, with whom I fell immediately in love. Suffice it to say, my momentary unwillingness to be very generous with views of this spectacle didn't endear me to people standing in line behind me. Charlie was impressed, too.

Before long our ship sailed out of San Francisco Bay and under the Golden Gate Bridge en route to Korea. As soon as we hit open water and the ocean's swells rocked the boat, our pleasant recollection of the night before was eradicated. We quickly learned what seasickness was.

The sea, however, wasn't always rough, and when it wasn't, we saw the beautiful flying fish. They were a gorgeous sight and their amazing ability to stay airborne as long as they did kept us entertained and grateful while we journeyed onward.

Finally, we reached Yokohama, Japan. We immediately disembarked, walked up the dock with our duffle bags and boarded another smaller troop ship. We were told that our ship was too large to enter Pusan Harbor in Korea; thus, we transferred to the smaller ship. Except for officers, no one was allowed to leave the ship, which would sail the next morning. Charlie Antle, Harold Baldwin, and I devised a scheme to get off the ship and visit Yokohama. All three of us were Sergeants First Class, giving us a little authority, and we presented ourselves to the MP guarding the gangway of our ship. I spoke to the MP, displayed my clipboard with the battery's equipment list, and pointed out to him that we needed to go back down the dock to the other ship and check on our equipment which was soon to unload, and ensure everything was in order. The MP agreed, we walked down the dock until we were out of sight, and free.

But not quite free. At the entrance to the dock area, there was a wide gate with Japanese guards, in this case checking the comings and goings of the dock area. Just as we were weighing this decision, many dockworkers began exiting the area in their typical faded work clothes and we had a plan. Crouching down in our dress uniforms among the smaller Japanese, we walked out with them.

Now we were free, and one of us had the inspiration to go to the U.S. Military Officers Club in the city where we could hook up with the Battalion Intelligence Officer, Capt. Charles Wilson, who was a friend of Charlie's. It was obvious we couldn't buy or visit anything in Yokohama if we didn't have a few dollars which we had long ago given up prior to our voyage. Fortunately, Capt. Wilson was the open-minded person we knew him to be and he gave us what we needed, including permission to be off the ship. From there it was all fun and games and we took full advantage of our good fortune.

So what did we do first? It's something of a blur, but we probably went first to the Seaman's Club, a place where sailors in Yokohama from all over the world gathered together for companionship, drink, food, and hospitality. We went in to have a drink, look around, enjoy the noise, and as luck would have it, meet some girls. We met a bevy of nice young Japanese women whose names I've forgotten, and enjoyed their company. Besides eating and drinking with our new friends, at some point we went shopping in a rickshaw and bought gifts for the ladies and for us to send home to girlfriends and mothers.

At a late hour we bade good night to our lady friends and headed back to the docks. There was no effort to hide our entrance into the dock area, as we knew nobody would detain us from heading to Korea where every person was needed at this point. The gate guards didn't even look at us when we passed by. But our bunkmates in the hold of our ship did gape at us when we returned with all the gifts and souvenirs, including a model boat for my youngest brother, cheap jewelry and other trinkets, and baubles. "How did you get off the ship?" was the first question, and the second was "Why didn't you take me?" We reveled in our temporary public acclaim and good fortune. The next day was back to the real world as we set sail for a land unknown to us and a strife that we couldn't envision.

Much can be said about this epic voyage and the enormity of the experience to go to Korea. But of our short, short visit in Yokohama, en route to Korea, I developed a profound respect and affection for the

Japanese people, whom I found to be intelligent, gentle, cultured, fun, and dedicated. So much did I enjoy the Japanese that I visited them twice again, including a visit with my late wife, during which I affirmed my respect and affection for them.

This appreciation of the Japanese extended to the Korean people with whom we worked during our engagement in Korea. We found both the Japanese and Korean people to be pleasant, dedicated, hard-working, and extremely grateful for the United Nations and American support for their countries.

MAM AND CONVERSE COLLEGE

Sally Parsonson

O ne of my thoughts in beginning to write memoirs was to produce accounts of the older generations, the family members I knew whom my children and grandchildren would never meet. So, this past week I opened a cardboard box marked "Things from Kosciusko" which I had tucked away after my mother's death in 1998. As the oldest child, I inherited the position of "Keeper of Family Records."

In this dusty box are photographs, many useless because they are undated and unidentified. "Why didn't I review this with my mother?" I ask myself. There are also letters, newspaper clippings, an envelope containing some Confederate dollar bills, and a small album into which someone, probably my grandmother, had pasted poems clipped from newspapers. At the bottom there are three fragile yearbooks from Converse College in Spartanburg, South Carolina: 1899, 1903, and 1904.

I have no idea why Mam, as I called my grandmother, kept the 1899 one. Perhaps it was given to her as admissions material since she had entered as a freshman in 1900. In contrast to the yearbooks of my school years, almost all the information and the pictures focus on the graduating class. Mam does not even appear in the 1903 edition. In the volume from 1904, her graduation year, I learned that she was the captain of the basketball team, a member of the North Carolina club and the YWCA, and participated in the senior play presented at graduation, Act V of Shakespeare's *A Midsummer Night's Dream*. She was a music major, one fact I did know, and had given a senior recital.

Next to Mam's cap-and-gown picture is a brief write-up: "The prima donna of the class. Beautiful brown eyes, red hair, and lovely dimples. The rushed of all the rushers. (*What does that mean?*) Wit is no name for her. Her favorite reading is "Life," and her favorite occupation is telling jokes, to which she always has to explain the point before her hearers can get up a laugh. She has recently entered the field of journalism and is achieving great success as a writer of love stories. She has a great affinity for small men."

"Who wrote this?" I wonder. I can verify the physical description: yes, she had beautiful hair which remained auburn even as her friends' hair grayed. And I know she wrote some published stories and kept journals, for I also have one of her journals from the 1940s in which she writes of my birth.

After graduation, she followed a friend from the 1903 class at Converse to become a schoolteacher in Kosciusko, Mississippi. She taught music in the public school for a few years until the music program was eliminated. She then turned to teaching American history for eighth-graders and gave private piano lessons after school. And she married a small man as the graduation note says she preferred. She always asserted that he was "the handsomest man in Kosciusko," even though he was no taller than she was.

As a child, I spent many summer weeks with her and Pop, my grandfather, in Kosciusko. The two of them had separate bedrooms, on opposite sides of the house. He smoked, which Mam never approved of. So until I was a teenager I slept with her in a big bed. Every night she would make up stories to tell me about a little girl named Lucy. During hot summer days we both spent many hours reading. She also helped me with piano lessons and encouraged me to practice. Every Sunday she took me with her to the First Methodist Church where she taught what she called "The Old Ladies' Sunday School Class." There was a piano in the classroom, and she always began class by playing upbeat hymns for the women to sing.

But what I remember most about music with her was how devoted she was to listening to the Metropolitan

Opera broadcasts on Saturday afternoon. She told me that her younger sister, Martha, whom she called Matt and who lived on Long Island, New York, might be at the opera performance. This was a weekly point of connection between the two of them, and, as a Christmas gift, Aunt Matt sent her a subscription to the *Opera News* annually. Once when Mam didn't have the opera score in her lap, I asked why she didn't sew or knit or do something with her hands while she was just listening. She quickly told me that listening to the opera WAS doing something. Music took all of her concentration. Of course now I wish I had inherited her concentration and learned more about the appreciation of music from her.

In that dusty box of materials, I learned a bit of family history that I had never heard discussed. And, having been a college administrator, I found it intriguing. I knew that Aunt Matt had moved north after her marriage and that her husband was a college professor who taught German. Also I knew that both sisters had graduated from Converse with Matt finishing two years after Mam. What I didn't know and found out from a newspaper clipping in the box was that Aunt Matt had, like Mam, moved to Kosciusko after graduation and had taught there for two years before she married. The brief article described a pre-wedding party for Matt before she left Kosciusko and briefly mentioned the man she was marrying. I was surprised to learn that he had been a professor at Wofford College, the men's college in Spartanburg, which was closely tied to Converse. Obviously, since Matt had moved to Mississippi, she must have known the professor while she was still a student. How did she get to meet him? Had they dated there? Had they fallen in love through letters after she graduated? Even in the 21st century fraternization between students and college teachers is taboo. But I'll never get to hear the full story. There are no living witnesses.

THE ICE CREAM SUNDAE INCIDENT

Beverly Baker

Kitchey and I worked the night shift at Pond's Ice Cream and Burger Shop when we were in high school. It was our first real job. We had done all sorts of other jobs together such as babysitting, dog walking, garden chores, and even set design for our school theater group, but this job was different since we were being paid a good minimum wage plus tips. We took the job seriously. When our friends came in to visit and sat at our counter stations, we would be sure to maintain our newly-found sense of professional decorum. I guess there was something about the starched uniforms and the little caps that kept us in line. Though, we did overindulge some of our customers like giving extra chocolate jimmies to the little kids and bigger scoops of ice cream to the nice jolly lady, Mrs. O'Brian, who came in every day at twilight—she left good tips. I looked expectantly toward the door and there she was, right on time, our first customer of the evening. The place was deserted because everyone was at the Neptune, New Jersey middle school playoff football game. It felt like the proverbial calm before the storm on that fall evening in 1957.

I adjusted my cap and apron and smiled a hello to her and hoped that she would choose my station. She seemed to know that she had to give equal time to each of us. I had served her the night before, so she waved to me and moved on to Kitchey's station. She was especially happy looking this evening because her grandchildren were coming to visit. I began to prepare my counter, wiping it down, and setting up some placemats. Henley, the short-order cook, came over to arrange the glassware in the shelves below the counter. He said, "You're going to need extras tonight for our sports fans. Our little hooligans will be expecting their rewards."

"I hope I can manage it, Henley. We might need your help."

"That will depend on how many burgers I need to flip."

"Where's Siegfried tonight?"

"Toilets—major leak—he's been on it all afternoon." Siegfried was the manager. He was a German-American graduate student in an art history Ph.D. program at Princeton. He was very nice to us, polite even though we knew he regarded us as clueless. We also knew that Henley was the real manager.

As I waited for the onslaught, I looked out the windows. It was dark now. I had the odd feeling of both being inside and outside at the same time. Inside it was warm and creamy yellow. It was an Art Deco styled building with curved tile walls and large plate glass windows facing Main Street. There was no moon tonight, and the street was empty, but the reflections of the interior were oddly projected on the windows. I thought the scene would make an interesting photograph. My reverie ended when the door opened with a bam. I was staring into the face of the obnoxious old man who complained about every sundae we made for him. I glanced at Kitchey and Mrs. O'Brian. They did not acknowledge his presence and kept on talking.

He chose to sit in the middle of my station directly in front of me. It could have been a snarl or a growl that I heard come out of him as he sat down and wrestled with his coat. I handed him the menu and said, "Good evening, Mr. Schmidt." He didn't look up at me, just uttered another grunt. He held the menu up to his very small gold-rimmed glasses, seemingly absorbed, as he perused the choices before he abruptly slammed it down. He looked at me with complete disdain. I shuddered and glanced toward Kitchey who, as usual, was ever mindful of my situation. I managed to smile at Mr. Schmidt who seemed to be gathering himself together. He began to speak in his most carefully constructed English-South African accent: "I shan't have anything unless I can have my favorite strawberry ice cream. It behooves me to say that you, young lady, are totally negligent for having taken it off the menu."

"Oh, but Mr. Schmidt, I don't have anything to do with the menu. I think it was something like a delivery problem—you know, breakdown or, I don't know, I'm sorry, I...."

"I know nothing about that—your problem. I only know what you are denying me what is the object of my desire." As he became more agitated, his accent began to change into something more foreign, more guttural, more like he usually spoke, and his face took on a blotchy purplish hue. He had the saltshaker in a death grip and was waving it at me.

I blurted out, "I'll call Siegfried. He will explain everything to you, and we'll come up with the perfect sundae, the sundae of your dreams!"

"I don't want something new! I want what I want! And that German manager—he's an idiot—I know them! Nazis!"

"Hi, Mr. Schmidt." It was Kitchey standing behind me, and Henley was a few feet behind her listening.

"You twit!" Schmidt spit out, "You gave me a bad sundae last time—you, you would not in my country be worthy of this job. You would be in the kitchen with the *swartzas*...."

"The what?" Kitchey asked. "He means the black people like me," said Henley. "Lord Have Mercy. I've got stuff on the grill." He ambled back to the kitchen, and we were left alone with the Thing from Hell who was suddenly quiet, even calm looking. I signaled to Kitchey, and we headed for her station. I whispered, "If only Siegfried were here."

"Actually, he hates Schmidt's guts. We need to fix this ourselves."

I said, "I'm not good with nut cases. Wait a minute. Mrs. O'Brian is a psychologist. She worked for years at Overbrook, the old asylum on the edge of town."

Mrs. O'Brian was not on her stool, but her coat was there. I nervously put my hand into my apron pocket and absently pulled out my dog's pink rubber ball. Kitchey gave me a wide-eyed look. "What's that?"

"Oh, nothing, just a dog ball. I throw it for Rex before I come here."

"EUREKA! This is it. We now have the perfect ingredient for the most marvelous sundae that Schmidt has ever experienced."

"Kitchey," I said in a warning tone. "We'll get fired. It's too risky." But I knew my friend had a huge capacity for the derring-do, and I loved being part of her antics. One time when we were painting the sets for our local teen theater production, she decided to spill some paint, step in it and walk on the canvas—her footprints making a path to the sky. The director got mad and told us to paint it out even though one of the songs was titled "Stairway to Heaven." Kitchey hummed the tune whenever she was near him, and I would chuckle.

We quickly placed the ball in the bottom of our fanciest parfait goblet. The ball was more perfect looking and rounder than any old scoop of ice cream could ever be. And, above all, it exuded expectation. (It reminded me of my four-year-old self when I made pretend mud brownies.) Our present creation only needed a little embellishment: a scoop of real ice cream, perhaps raspberry, garnished with chocolate sauce and adorned with a huge mound of whipped cream and extra jimmies plus the perfect cherry crown.

We presented it to Mr. Schmidt, who was by now practically foaming at the mouth for lack of attention. "What is this?" he demanded. A big galumph-like sound emanated from his mouth. For a few seconds he almost seemed pleased. He daintily tasted the raspberry and chocolate mix—umm, he murmured. Then he dug a little deeper and practically spooned up the whole raspberry scoop. Then he really dug down to the bottom and felt resistance. His little piggy eyes narrowed, "What the hell?" He raised his head like a wounded animal and was about to bellow, but at that moment the door slammed open against the tile as the football warriors burst into the shop.

The great throng of little people swarmed through the not-too-spacious soda fountain aisles, jostling one another, laughing, shouting, and boasting about their victory while bashing carelessly into Schmidt. His sundae went over. The ball rolled out onto the counter. One of the Tucker twins snatched it up, and they all began tossing it about.

At that point, Mrs. O'Brian threaded her way through the throng toward Schmidt. She had a vague sense of being in the asylum again. When she reached him, she said, "It's time to go home. I'll walk with you."

He looked at her as though she was an apparition and simultaneously began to shout as she led him away: "You have tricked me! I'm going to sue! I'm not paying!"

Mrs. O'Brian held his arm tightly as she steered him toward the door. The cashier let them pass by without so much as a glance.

Kitchey and I were still slammed. This event would last till closing time, ten o'clock. I looked at the clock— one half hour to go, and now the kids and their few escorts were leaving. There was a sense of "the party's over, let's call it a day." We breathed a sigh of relief except for the fact that Siegfried was standing there with his arms folded and looking stern. "Well, girls, how did it go tonight?"

I remember stammering, and Kitchey interrupted me with, "Schmidt was here—very demanding...." I added, "Nasty, insulting, especially to Henley."

"Yes, yes. When I got here, I just saw the kids tossing the ball and keeping it away from Schmidt. I don't know where the ball came from and why Schmidt was so keen on trying to get the ball. I've been fixing toilets all day. My thesis is due in two weeks. I don't have time to interview new candidates for your jobs. The best thing is to promote Henley. He deserves it. People like Schmidt are afraid of authority: they are bullies. Henley will have the added responsibility of being in charge of customer relations. He's been here a long time. The owners depend upon him. They live in Florida where they are starting a new restaurant. They have asked me to go down there if I want to. A long time ago, during the war, a member of their family enabled my family to escape from Germany just in time. Life's connections are tight. Oh, dear, I am forgetting how young and innocent you two are—well, I do know how zany and devious you can be, how creative. I just study art and try to decipher it. Maybe I should study culinary art and make something for a change."

He abruptly said good night and added, "I expect you to be here tomorrow night, right on time, uniforms in order, and double-check the ice cream sundae manual before you make one."

As it turned out, we did realize that we were experiencing a lucky moment. Siegfried had every right to fire us, but his world view was larger than his job description, and he was wrestling with his future options. We, too, would be facing new choices and opportunities. We both made the cheerleading squad in our junior year and were elevated to "hot stuff" —for all that's worth. Pond's became a much lauded and enriching memory. Oftentimes, we stopped in to see Henley who as the official manager sported a collared shirt and tie under his chef jacket, and he wore his new authority with genteel aplomb. Pond's business was booming.

Over the years, we learned that Siegfried did go to Miami and became one of the new celebrity chefs to open a chain of international restaurants. But more importantly, the Sundae Incident at Pond's made us realize forever that there's nothing like a second chance and, also, that you have to choose the people you move through life with very carefully.

Alcatraz

Carolyn Fore

The summer I was 13 years old, my family drove across the United States and visited every site there was to see, or at least that's what it seemed like to a 13-year-old who suffered from car sickness. We did see a lot of the country in a short time as we started from our home in Pittsburgh, Pennsylvania as soon as school was out and drove to Boothbay Harbor, Maine, then returned to Pittsburgh and began our journey to California. We stopped at landmarks along the way as we drove day after day and charted our course to be certain we found historic or otherwise interesting stops. One of my favorites was massive Mount Rushmore followed by the beautifully scenic Badlands of South Dakota. This trip occurred before there were interstate highways going every direction and McDonald's on practically every street corner, so we carefully plotted our path on the highway system and packed food for sandwiches into a cooler in the backseat of the car, tucked away under my feet. My family had a big Cadillac with lots of room in the back and, since my legs were short, there was room for the cooler under my legs. Besides, half the time I was lying down on my half of the seat sleeping through my car sickness.

Once we arrived in California, we settled into the rental house we occupied for a month in the quaint town of Lone Pine, where my father was working on contract negotiations. This was a classic 60s small town nestled in the mountains where the TV show "Have Gun Will Travel" was filmed. My father loved that TV show. I have a picture of him with the star of the show, Paladin, played by Richard Boone, both wearing their cowboy hats.

While in Lone Pine, we traveled to different parts of California. For my sister's twentieth birthday, near the end of July, we went to San Francisco to spend the weekend. We celebrated her birthday with dinner at the Top of the Mark restaurant, which was on the top floor of the Mark Hopkins Hotel. It was a cold, foggy, summer day in San Francisco, and while we had a great view of San Francisco Bay, it was difficult to decipher what we were looking at. We had been there long enough to figure out the lay of the land when a family came by, and in a loud, obnoxious, New York accent the mom in the group said repeatedly to her children, "Look, look over there, a big ship, do you see the big ship?"

She even leaned over our table and pointed at it. My parents, my sister, and I looked at each other giggling, and could hardly contain our outburst of laughter until they walked out of hearing range. Finally, we let loose as we all said at the same time, "That's not a ship, that's Alcatraz." That became a family joke for many years afterwards.

That was 1961, just two years before Alcatraz closed as a prison. I didn't see Alcatraz again until 1998 when my daughter and her husband were living in San Francisco. On one of many visits to see them we decided to take the tour of Alcatraz. In 1961 when there were still prisoners living there, it was a scary looking, off-limits place. By 1998 the former prison was a tourist attraction. My adrenalin was already in high gear when I got on the boat to cross the bay to go to the island. I could hardly believe we could now visit the place Al Capone and so many other famous prisoners had been imprisoned. Stepping off the boat was like stepping back in time. Nothing had changed and the feeling was a combination of going back to the past and feeling haunted. As I walked around the grounds, I could almost hear the echoes of voices shouting out orders to prisoners. Once inside, the atmosphere was dark and dreary. The smells of the past overwhelmed me. The ghosts of prisoners seemed to have stayed behind when the cells were vacated. I was uncomfortable and anxious to get back to the open air. I could only imagine the life of the prisoners who had once called these eerie, bleak hallways and cells home. Even the staff quarters weren't very appealing. And to think that some of the staff had their families living there with them. It was hard to process my feelings of such a place.

CAIRO

Stefan Fatzinger

B y the time I arrived at the hotel in Cairo, the flight, airport, and drive into the city had exhausted me, and I was sure that I would sleep well that night before having to visit my clients the following day.

The next morning I approached the front desk to inquire about hiring a car for the day. "With or without a driver?" was the reply. Remembering the taxi ride from the airport and the traffic chaos I had encountered, I responded, "What is the price with a driver?" I was astounded by the answer: "$30." "For the entire day?" "Yes." And so, without hesitation, for the first time in my life, I hired not only a car but a driver to go along with it, a young Egyptian who spoke remarkably good English.

Providing him with the addresses of the day's business destinations, I sat back and let my senses reveal to me the smells, sounds, and sights of this ancient city. The driver was so efficient that by 2:30

in the afternoon I was finished with my business for the day. When my new-found companion asked me what our next destination would be, the thought that had been germinating in my mind since about noon exploded from my lips, "Can we visit the pyramids?" "Of course," was the reply, and off we went.

As we were driving through Cairo on our way to Giza, the driver pointed to a crowd of people milling about at an intersection and said, "That is one of my friends. May I pick him up and give him a ride?" I was beginning to enjoy myself to such an extent and was looking with such anticipation to seeing the pyramids that without giving it another thought, I readily consented. The two "friends" conversed for a few minutes in the front seats in Egyptian while I continued to soak in my surroundings. Then the friend turned around and asked me in English if I would like to ride a camel to the pyramids. I smiled and thanked him for the offer and, opening my wallet which contained only ten Saudi Riyal (about $2), advised him that I had no money and therefore could not pay for such an adventure. (I never carried cash on an international trip; I only used credit cards.) He smiled and retorted, "That is no problem. You don't have to pay anything." I said, "Okay, but can I ride a camel in a three-piece suit and tie?" "Not a problem."

And then an amazing thing happened. One moment we were in the city, and the next, without any warning or other signs, we were in the desert. Cairo just ended and the desert began. The car pulled up to a small building on the edge of the Sahara, and there in front of the small structure were four camels lying on the sand being tended by a twelve- or thirteen-year-old boy. We got out of the car, and I was led to one of the camels and instructed on how to mount this extraordinary animal. Feeling a little ridiculous in my three-piece suit and tie, I climbed on my camel and was then told that the young boy would grab the reins that circled the creature's head and lead my ride for the afternoon. The driver remained with the car while his "friend" climbed on one of the two remaining camels and joined the boy and me as we rode off into the desert. Not long into our journey we came upon three gentlemen clothed in Arab dress, and I was asked if I wanted a Coca-Cola and a Keffiyeh, the traditional Arab headdress. I once again responded that I had no money, but my guide responded, "Just give them the ten Saudi Riyal in your wallet." I smiled at his remarkable memory and did as instructed.

So now I sat on a camel in a three-piece suit and tie with a Keffiyeh on my head and a Coca-Cola in my hand. Lawrence of Arabia, eat your heart out! For the next hour or so we rode our camels across the sand, witnessing such sights as the Ramesses' statues guarding Memphis, before coming upon the Great Sphinx of Giza which guards the massive pyramids of Khufu (Cheops), Khafre (Chephren), and Menkaure

(Mycerinus). I was mesmerized. My breath was taken away as what I had only seen in two-dimensional pictures became a three-dimensional reality. I had to pinch myself to realize it was not all just a dream. After spending about fifteen minutes admiring the Sphinx, we next rode our camels around the three large pyramids before I dismounted from my camel and was given instructions on how best to climb inside and explore Khufu. I spent the next hour going back thousands of years in time as I descended, climbed, and squeezed my way through narrow passageways exploring this remarkable tomb. One of my most memorable observations was the smell of urine that still a millennia later held its pungent ammonia odor. As I exited the tomb, my camel and new friends were waiting for me. We all remounted our camels and rode back to the little shack where this magnificent experience had begun.

As I dismounted my camel, I turned to the guide and said, "This has been one of the best days of my life. Thank you so very much for this marvelous experience! My only regret is that I don't have any money to be able to pay you." "That's okay," he responded. "We take credit cards." I began to chuckle and then to laugh heartily. I had been had, or had I? Would I have enjoyed myself as much as I had, had the circumstances been any different? I doubt it seriously. "How much?" I asked. "Whatever you think it was worth," he responded. As the Visa commercials suggest, my adventure was "priceless." And so I walked into the small shack at the edge of the desert and spent several hundred dollars, not regretting one penny.

Rafting with Friends

Carolyn Fore

The mention of river rafting usually takes me back to childhood memories of summers at Garner State Park near Boerne, Texas. However, one more recent experience in North Georgia gave me a completely different perspective. A friend of mine who has a cabin somewhere between Ellijay and Jasper invited six ladies to spend the day enjoying the mountain scenery while relaxing in the quiet surroundings. We arrived at her cabin mid-morning and enjoyed a picnic lunch on the screened-in porch overlooking the woods, the mountains, and a peaceful river. After sufficient eating and socializing, our hostess said she had plenty of rafts for us to get out on the river, so off we went.

We put our rafts, which were simply old inner tubes, in the river at a small bridge crossing where our hostess dropped us off, and we were joyously on our way as carefree as kids. It wasn't long before we were all separated, but we were smart enough to stay in groups of two. Katie and I were having a delightful time moseying down the river and talking about everything in the world from who we had seen recently to how beautiful the mountains were. Then we hit some debris in the river which must have accumulated with the excess rain the week before. We tried to keep pushing sticks out of our way, but somehow one punctured my inner tube, and before I knew what happened, I was hanging on to flat black rubber. I yelled to Katie since we were staying together but not right beside each other, and she paddled toward me in her inner tube as I started swimming toward her. We went a little farther down the river with me desperately hanging on to her inner tube as the current seemed to be picking up.

We finally decided to make our way to the riverbank where I got out and started walking, but Katie wanted to stay in the water. The walking wasn't easy, and I tried to stay even with Katie for safety reasons for both of us. We were both starting to get a little concerned about our situation and wondering where we were but knew that the river would eventually take us back to our friend's cabin. But how far away was it?

Finally, we heard voices yelling "Katie, Carolyn, Katie, Carolyn" over and over. We yelled back "Here we are." Then there was "Where are you?" We answered "Here we are!" until we finally connected with our friends.

We were very glad to see them, but they seemed even more relieved to see us, especially our hostess. I explained what happened to my inner tube, and Katie got out of the water. Then we said we hoped we were near the cabin. They started explaining how they had been frantically searching for us.

Right after we started rafting, they found out that water was being let out of the dam, and everyone was supposed to get out of the river in that area. No rafting was allowed that day. We didn't see the signs because of where we jumped in, but the others hadn't taken off right away and someone stopped them before they even got in the water. For the past hour they had been in a panic that something had happened to us and were almost to the point of reporting it to the rangers to get help searching for us.

Many years later we still laugh about the rafting incident when we see each other.

PART FOUR

"Kinda Soggy"

Jeannie Longley

Our family grew up camping and hiking, as my father was a lover of exercise and the great outdoors. Although I sometimes railed against some of the hikes, particularly in the dead of winter in Illinois, I too grew to love these activities. Lester, my husband, shares this love, and consequently our children grew up camping and hiking. Like me, my daughter Dori protested greatly as a child, but not long after she left for college, I came across a college essay of hers which I had never seen. The topic related to writing about something that the writer claimed to hate, but in fact liked. Lo and behold, she'd written about hiking.

One memorable trip included not just the four of us, but also my parents. My parents had graduated to what my children referred to as Grandma and Grandpa's "car house," a small motor home, but the four of us were in a tent. We headed north to a small lake created by the Civilian Conservation Corps called Lake Conasauga. It is in a remote area of Georgia, and the final approach involves a drive of several miles on a gravel road. The trip is worth it: the views are stunning, the songbirds provide a constant chorus, and the wildlife is abundant. In fact, after retiring the first night we were there, we could hear bears trying to get into the garbage bins not far away.

The next day we decided to go for a hike in another area of the Cohutta Wilderness, a short drive away on the Jacks River Trail. The trail was steep and narrow in parts, and, although my father had used a cane for decades, he was spry, and the trek would have normally not been a challenge.

What we didn't anticipate was that a terrific storm was approaching with a torrential downpour, golf-ball-sized hail, thunder, lightning, and wind. There we were in the middle of the forest with no place to hide. Anticipating the difficulty of getting back, Dori and I prayed for a safe return, and I remember thinking at one point that if we were going to die, we were going to die. My father had a long-standing acrophobia, and the only way he could walk at that point was to crabwalk sideways on the trail, so he didn't have to look down. We eventually made it back to our car and to the campsite, thoroughly drenched and exhausted.

Being ever the efficient packer, my husband had brought only the jeans he was wearing, so we all piled into the car and headed into nearby Ellijay for new pants at the local Walmart, and barbecue at the Pink Pig, followed by ice cream at the Dairy Queen before we returned to our campground

Later on during our stay, we chatted with a couple who had been coming to the campground for twenty-five years. They told us they had had only one trip when there had not been a downpour. They attributed these frequent rains to the Eastern Continental Divide. They had long ago renamed the lake "Kinda Soggy."

THE BOATING PARTY

Christy Baker Knight

"Here, you gotta try these—best in Miami." Captain Luis shoved the giant box of Cuban pastries our way.

"Mm, thank you, I already ate but will definitely have one later." I knew to be careful on a boat, especially with the sketchy weather forecast; the tropical May sun was supposed to get blotted out by a storm. Our twelve-year-old daughter, Bev, didn't hesitate though, and Luis nodded proudly as she enjoyed the treat.

"You want one?" I asked my husband, Michael, who wore a bucket hat for the sun. He had arranged our vacation in Miami and this three-hour tour as part work trip and part elementary school graduation gift to Bev. "Absolutely." He selected a pastry and nibbled on it. "Incredible."

"Up, two more passengers." Luis beckoned a couple onto his tiny craft. "Welcome aboard *Bambino*."

"Mornin' Captain," the young girl with leadership qualities called. She and a guy with the faintest scruff of red beard made strong handshakes with him as they boarded. Our knees bumped from the new cargo as they chatted with Captain Luis in sailing lingo I didn't understand. This flat-topped motorboat wasn't like any sailboat I'd ever seen. Could we all fit? We'd chosen the more spacious open seating in the back, and now it looked like we would be awkwardly jammed in.

"We're still waiting on one more passenger. Have a Cuban pastry, best in Miami," Luis nudged. She helped herself and extended the box for red beard. "Eh, no thanks."

"No?" the girl with navy shorts and ink on her hip held a powdered-sugar bomb up anyway, as if to change his mind.

"Told ja I partied way too much last night." Red beard slinked into a deck cushion. He said to us, "I'm Justin, and the loud one's Carley." At the helm, Carley was getting nautical with the Captain, pointing to the controls and asking questions.

We introduced ourselves back. "You guys ever seen an ocean race before?" Michael asked them as a cloud swooped over, blocking the sun. Justin's eyes followed the same color change as the water, from the Brisk Blue I'd painted Bev's room to ominous Gunmetal. Michael hadn't but knew all about the race due to work in the manufacturing of the high-performance sails.

"Me neither," Justin said. "We're from a sailing club in Toronto. I can't wait to see the teamwork in action. The trust it takes to crew an ocean race is epic."

After Luis passed Carley's full inspection of *Bambino*, firm handshakes went around. "Dude, we're gonna miss the race," Carley said, loud enough for our captain to hear.

"I know," Michael checked his phone. "Starts in less than an hour and it'll take us that long to get out of the bay."

"Hold on folks, I think this is our guy," Luis said. A small hairy-armed man with a backpack approached the boat, and Captain signaled for him to board.

"Soddy I'm late," he said in a high-pitched voice. "I'm Hector. Nice to meet ju." He sat in the covered shade while the rest of us braved the sun, hats locked down tight.

"That's six passengers; we're good to go." Luis said. Hector wasn't even offered a Cuban pastry before Luis pulled his pride and joy away from the dock. We motored out of the marina, passing a tiki bar. Two shark surf boards had holes tourists could stick their faces in for cheesy photos. We tuned into a local station offering hot hits all weekend long.

Cruising through the glassy bay, you could tell Luis enjoyed hauling tourists around the ritzy mansions. "This one's owned by Tony Camino, ever heard of him?"

We shook our heads as he listed the sports teams, restaurants, and cars the said tycoon owned. "He made a *fortune*. A long time ago, I was his bodyguard. Anyway, see these homes, every one of em's worth *millions*."

"Jes, Meellions," Hector confirmed. He sounded like Fez in *That '70s Show*. But the Canadians didn't seem impressed by the moguls dripping in wealth. Instead, they spread out on the deck and caught some rays. Justin teased Carley about her savage tan being the color of egg salad. Luis raised his voice as he pointed into the swampy trees rimming the bay. "And see that place ova' there, I worked for that guy too, worth a ton."

"Meellions and meellions," Hector nodded in agreement.

"But wait'll you see the next one." Luis slowed the motor so we could gawk at a modern deal with lots of glass. "Now this mansion, it's kind of different but don't let that fool ya—*mucho dinero*, you know what I'm saying?"

"Meellions and meellions of dollars," Hector said while circling his wrist high in the air for emphasis. But the ocean race wasn't being held anywhere near the mansions of the rich and famous. As they shrunk behind us, the bay turned wicked silver. A dark line on the horizon told us we were heading directly into the storm.

Leaving Biscayne Bay, it wasn't clear if Luis had ever boated beyond his easy-chair tourist route, and

Michael left us for the helm to help with directions to the ocean race. The waves kicked up so fast it was like climbing into a trampoline when three people are already jumping around. I stood to grab a metal pole. The only passenger wearing a life vest, Bev stayed in her seat, and, entering the uncharted territory of middle school parenting, I wanted to protect but celebrate her independence whenever possible. I was grateful when she eventually joined me at the pole, our ballast amid the thrashing chaos.

The Canadians took our empty seats. They flailed but, like seasoned subway riders, continued conversations and even sipped drinks around each bump and jarring jolt. The sky had settled on a color, Dementor Gray, and the sea accented the choice with a bold flooring of Black Abyss. Boats appeared like new furniture. One stained-wood vessel displayed a yellow and blue Swedish flag. A large tour boat ironically promised tranquil waters, and a yacht bullied its way onto the scene. Like a junky family heirloom no one dares get rid of, *Bambino* was noticeably the wimpiest craft.

The horizon swayed up and down. When the box of pastries went flying off the center table, Bev tugged at my arm, the one not attached to the pole. "Mom?" She looked at me.

I knew that face. *Oh-no.* "Look all around, honey," I offered. Despite avoiding the pastries, I wasn't feeling too spectacular either.

"Breathe deeply," Michael yelled from the helm, cluing in to the blue-cheese tint of Bev's face. But she was already moonwalking to a seat with easy access to feeding the fish. Mama instincts won and I bumped my way over to hold her (and her hair).

"Dude, now who looks like egg salad?" Carley shouted to Justin who had turned his own queasy shade of mold. The boat swayed hideously with each wave from the wake of larger ships knocking us around. The horizon went up and down, up and down, up and down like a maniacal see-saw.

"Shut up," he said and put his head down. But soon Justin made it to the other side of the boat and puked into the waves. I fought the urge to join them. It was a source of pride, my strong stomach, but the thought of egg salad and aroma of acidic vomit weren't helping. To thwart the tugging sensation on my gut, I tuned in to the race chat. Michael liked to talk shop about the technical wares he sold that went into the sails, and now he had the perfect audience.

"The cost it takes to rig one of these boats is unbelievable," Luis said.

"Amazing that wicked expensive sails are only used once," Carley added.

"Meellions and meellions," Hector agreed.

"You seen an ocean race before?" Luis asked Hector.

"Jes, I'm following thee race around thee world, reporting for my yacht club een Veracruz." He put the binoculars back up to peer at the tiny sails on the horizon. The racers circled in a warm-up lap. Tall splashes of electric orange, teal, and crimson popped in the Black Abyss.

The sail holding an octopus graphic reminded me that, like the Kraken, this storm could take us down any minute. "Do they ever call this thing off?" I shouted into the wind.

Justin smoothed out his beard. "Yeah, sometimes they say, okay doesn't look good. Let's just have some beers."

"Okay, Beers!" Hector squeaked.

"Beers!" The Canadians boomed.

"Check out that beauty," Justin whistled while holding on. "She's a real catch!"

"Don't you mean a ketch?" Carley corrected. "As in type of sailboat."

"That too."

The elegant craft glided across the current, cutting a path through the muck of worker boats. Her shellacked wood frame was accessorized with every kind of fancy rigging money could buy, and the crew looked equally put together. A photographer on board steadied his professional lens on the race while a gray-haired guy—whose picture could qualify under the definition of Captain—stood at the helm. The vessel might have belonged to one of the mansion owners Luis and Hector had drooled over.

I honed in on the name bolted to the side: *Royal Flush*. She sliced through yards of lashing waves. "I bet whoever owns that's worth millions," Luis said to Hector. *Royal Flush* didn't stick around to see our reaction. She slipped past the traffic now clogging the route. Flags snapped as hulls dipped precariously through the choppy waves. Everyone was headed in the same direction but somehow managing to keep enough distance between our rocking rides not to play bumper boats.

Bev was feeling well enough to stand again, and we held on to our pole together. The rhythm was easier to calculate now, and even when a large yacht cruised the perimeter, we braced ourselves for the rolling wake that followed. The sun came out for a moment of Brisk Blue.

"What's the word on the race? Is it happening?" Michael asked as Luis maneuvered our wild ride through the crowd. Most of the circling sails had gone down in the warm-up lap.

"Might call it off, we'll tune in and see." Our captain sounded a little panicked as *Bambino* swayed back and forth in the violent swells. A concentrated expression crossed his profile when he turned to check the distance between us and a fishing boat. Luis elbowed his way up a notch in traffic. *Bambino* swayed and jerked as a sleek hull bobbed beside us. We had made it to the lunch table where *Royal Flush* held court.

The storm and all the wakes spun massive waves. *Bambino* tilted precariously, careening at a sharp angle. Each time we swung high to the left and right, I urged Bev to hold on tight and could feel calluses form. Adrenaline set in as I feared we would keel over.

"Whoa, what the!" Captain Luis shouted. *Royal Flush* cut too close. Time slowed under pressure. We were suspended in animation as something horrific flashed. Luis turned to get away from *Royal Flush*, but she swung hard. *Bambino* thrashed as her nose headed straight into that polished wood hull. Her captain shouted and waved his arms from the helm.

Luis was straining as the Canadians called out helpful suggestions. We were about to get royally flushed. Impact was not optional, as we braced for the inevitable. The perfect-looking captain of *Royal Flush* ran on the deck directly into the point of contact. He continued to shout at us, but this time he used his body as a blockade. He stuck out his leg and pushed us back with an arm. I heard the crunch of hulls and maybe bone as the rigging hit his head. He pulled back in pain as expletives sounded from our unlikely crew.

With the help of the Canadians, Luis unhinged his bow from *Royal Flush* and was backing up and away as far as possible in the churning mess of vessels. We worked our way fast to the fringes of society.

"Dude, can you believe that idiot?" Carley said.

"Seriously," Justin added. "Any sailor knows you never leave the helm in a conflict."

"And you never deflect the blow with your body!" Carley yelled.

The Canadians shouted together, "You never *ever* deflect the blow!"

Hector mimicked their war cry. "Never deflect thee blow!"

"I think I know that boat." Luis took off his hat and raked a hand through what little hair he had. "We'll go find it at the other marina and see what we can do. Sorry about this, folks."

"Man, what an idiot that guy was," Carley said. "The most stupid mistake I've ever seen. Hasn't he read the rule book?"

"Well, we were in a collision so the thing to do is resolve the conflict," Luis said.

"Absolutely," Carley agreed. "And while we're checking on him, why don't we tell that jerk how stupid he was to deflect the blow!"

When we made it back to the bay, the ride smoothed out enough for us to lounge like lazy tourists. We passed a few mega-mansions, but Luis didn't say a word about who owned them as we braced for our meeting with *Royal Flush*.

This marina was larger than where *Bambino* docked. "Lotta nice boats in here," Luis said as we motored around the yacht parking lot. "Okay, we check on him, make sure he's okay, and then we—"

"—tell him what a stupid idiot he was to think a human leg could stop a freaking boat!" Carley yelled.

"He's totally at fault here," Justin said.

"I just hope he's okay." Luis turned down the radio. "You know I have a bad feeling about this."

"That guy broke so many rules, and we have witnesses," I reassured him.

"We're with you, Captain," Carley said.

"Guns ready," Michael said.

"Yeah, bring out the bazookas!" The Canadians cheered.

"Bring out dee ba-dookas!" Hector squeaked as we passed row after row of fancy rigging.

Royal Flush taunted us from the dock. Her captain emerged from the cabin alone, wearing an arm sling and a bandage on his forehead. I'm pretty sure he was limping too.

"Are you all right, Sir?" Luis asked from yards below.

"*You* hit my boat, and I think I have a broken arm. Do you realize how much damage you've done?! You'll be hearing from my lawyer."

"Sir, that's not necessary, is it? I came to find you and I'll give you my insurance information."

"You bet you will, and you'll never captain that boat again."

"Hey, you're at fault for leaving the helm and deflecting the blow with your body!" Carley yelled. The Canadians stood behind Luis. Michael and I did our best impressions of intimidating thugs, Bev mimicking us with crossed arms and a scowl. Hector flew from his perch and mirrored the protective stance of priceless bodyguards.

"Listen, do you have any idea how expensive this ship is to sail? And I had clients on board," the wounded captain said.

"So does he, your royal flushing hiney!" Carley yelled.

Luis was silent.

"That thing?" the Captain said, looking at *Bambino* like she was last year's bargain-bin knock off.

"Sir," Luis said. "I asked if you're all right and I can meet with you tomorrow to settle this in a professional manner."

"Fine." The captains opened their wallets to exchange cards.

Luis had managed to salvage some pastries from the smashed box. No one looked like they were going to puke, so we spread out the picnics we'd packed, sharing hummus, carrots, and cheese cubes as a snack frenzy began.

"You guys, thank you for standing up for me and *Bambino*." Luis was touched—still sweating from possibly losing his livelihood—but touched.

"Of course, we always stand with our captain!" Carley raised her cup.

"Yeah, especially when some idiot deflects the blow." As if Justin needed to remind us.

"Here's to Luis, our fearless leader and the best damned captain ever!" we cheercd. Michael and I joined in the toast as Bev sipped her water. "Okay, Beers!" We clunked solo cups.

"Beers! To Luis and *Bambino*." The evening light was golden, the water calm as silk, as we cruised back to the marina.

The Panama Canal

Carolyn Fore

I woke up early, anticipating the excitement the day had in store for us. I had opened my eyes at 5 a.m. and realized the ship had stopped and the sun was rising, but now at 6, I was ready to get up and see what was happening outside. Our massive cruise ship was drifting at the entrance to the Panama Canal. The tugboats swirled around us, positioning to escort us into the first lock. Workers scurried along the pathways beside the first lock, making sure everything was ready. At 7 a.m. our captain's voice resounded over the speaker system letting us know that with all inspections and official paperwork completed we were cleared to move into the locks. The engines roared again.

As if in slow motion, we started moving forward into the blocked-off area that was the first of three locks on the eastern side of the Panama Canal. We continued to move forward until we were almost touching the gate that separated the first and second locks. Then we felt the ship jolt to a stop, and there was an air of excitement as the thick ropes were thrown to the sides to anchor us. The gate behind the rear of the ship gradually closed. During this time, people on the ship were hanging over their balconies taking pictures while at the same time, the workers on the ground were finding time to take pictures of our gigantic ship. It was also quite exciting for the locals since our cruise ship, the Norwegian Bliss, was the largest passenger ship, the second largest ship, to go through the Panama Canal. It created quite a stir.

Once we were tethered in place, the sound of the water filling the lock bellowed. At first it was difficult to tell that the water level was rising, but gradually it became evident that we were reaching the level of the next lock, approximately 28 feet higher than we had started. It would be necessary for us to go up 85 feet total in the three locks. After our water level reached the top marks, the swirling of incoming water stopped and the gate between the first and second lock slowly opened. The engines started roaring again. We were untethered from the sides and slowly moved into the second lock. Then the process started all over again in the second lock and repeated one more time in the third lock.

When we exited this set of locks, we entered the calm, scenic water of Lake Gatun. I was surprised to see at least eight ships patiently waiting to enter the two sets of locks going toward the Atlantic Ocean, the direction we had just come from. There was also a cruise ship ahead of us that we had been able to see going through the locks before us.

A quick explanation of how the Panama Canal is structured may be helpful. At both coasts there are three sets of locks that raise the ships 85 feet to allow them to go across the Isthmus of Panama through the country of Panama. Traversing from the Atlantic Ocean side, the locks empty into Lake Gatun, a man-made lake, allowing ships to cross over it in about three hours. Then the ships enter the Chagres River, which was dammed to create the lake, and becomes a channel leading to the locks on the Pacific Ocean side where the ships are lowered 85 feet back to sea level in a reverse, three-lock process. The original canal was finished in 1914, but the expansion project to build a wider set of locks for bigger ships was completed in 2016. We went through the newer channel built by the expansion project and could see other ships entering and exiting the older locks. Lake Gatun and the Chagres River are designated as protected rainforest areas because the balance of water is essential to keeping the locks functioning.

When we reached the entrance to the locks on the Pacific side, we were again stopped for an official inspection. We were also told that Panamanian dignitaries were boarding for a ceremony acknowledging this was the largest cruise ship ever to go through the canal. We watched a television news reporter with his cameraman reporting from the dock below our balcony. Once we were cleared to continue, we went through the locks, similar to the process we had gone through earlier in the day, except in reverse; starting with the lock full of water, we watched it drain out before moving to the next one. As we went through the three sets of locks, it was getting dark and from the port side of our ship we could see Panama City starting to glow as the lights came on. As we left the last lock and headed out to the Pacific Ocean, the ship picked up speed, and we waved good-bye to Panama as we headed off to dinner marveling about our 12-hour transit across Panama.

CRUISING INTO TEREZIN

Tony Clarke

The scenic Rhine River cruise my brother and I took in the first week of August 2016 terminated in a visit to Prague. Prague is the beautiful and historical capital city of the Czech Republic, a country formed from the divestment of Slovakia from Czechoslovakia in 1993. We arrived on a Monday afternoon in Prague after leaving Vienna, Austria, early, touring Bratislava, Slovakia, later, and finally arriving in Prague in the late afternoon. What's remarkable about this day starting in Vienna, and on to Bratislava and Prague, is our being in three European capital cities in the same day. This was an Olympic-style achievement that had been carefully orchestrated.

Prague proved to be the beautiful, must-see, city everybody had told us. Two days were spent walking the historical downtown, the old city, which is unique in that so much history is concentrated in that smaller downtown area. It's easy to walk, in spite of all the cobblestones, and is unusually dramatic. Almost half of one day was spent, after walking across the stone pedestrian bridge, the Charles Bridge (named after Charles IV), over the Vatic River visiting the Prague Castle. The castle included the magnificent St. Vitus Church, the Bishop's Palace, and a monastery. There was a lot to see, and as the day progressed, the crowds grew larger with longer lines forming to pass through the checkpoints staffed by armed police.

For the first two days in Prague we had spectacular weather, sunshine with balmy temperatures. Our third and last day in Prague was foreboding with dark clouds, light rain, and a chill in the air. This harsher weather started during our bus trip some 40 miles to Terezin, a small fortress town from the late 18th century that came into strategic importance in the wars between the Habsburg Empire and Prussia. From the 19th century part of the fortifications, the Small Fortress was used as a prison for military and political convicts. In the late 1930s, however, the use of the Small Fortress was further expanded as a prison for political prisoners of the Nazi regime which had occupied Bohemia and Moravia in Czechoslovakia.

Later, the further expansion of Terezin, the whole town, into one big prison, a ghetto in effect, took place in 1941 when a plan was devised as part of the Final Solution by Reinhard Heydrich, the Deputy Reich Protector, also known as The Hangman. Incidentally

Heydrich was mortally wounded in May 1942 by two soldiers of the Czech Free Army who parachuted into Czechoslovakia from their base in London. The two soldiers and many innocent civilians were killed following Heydrich's death. His idea envisioned isolating the Jews from the general population, concentrating them in a few areas, and then sending them off to the East for their liquidation. In effect, Terezin was to be a collection point for Jews from everywhere after which they would be sent east to Auschwitz and other extermination camps in eastern Europe.

Terezin, a small walled town, was easily guarded with barrack buildings capable of holding many people. It was accessible by rail and road and had SS and other guard units already there. Thus, it became an ideal concentration camp. The first transports of Jews and other prisoners arrived on November 24, 1941 (the day before my eleventh birthday). One hundred forty thousand people were sent to Terezin during World War II of whom 110,000 died: 33,000 at Terezin itself, primarily from disease and starvation, and 87,000 in Eastern extermination camps.

Stepping off the bus into the rain, we dodged muddy puddles. Although Terezin receives a large number of tourists, it hasn't been furnished like many tourist sites with asphalt or cobblestone walkways, and the rain gathered in puddles. The overriding gloom of the day contributed to the foreboding atmosphere when we went first through the Jewish Cemetery, then into the crematorium buildings. Our first view was of the four oil-powered incinerators. Of the 30,000 prisoners cremated at Terezin, most had died of disease and starvation. Only a few executions were carried out at Terezin.

Corpses were placed in the incinerators without coffins so the coffins could be reused for transporting bodies. The workers operated the incinerators diligently to get all the human remains out and place them properly in urns. These urns went into the columbarium in the fortress walls, except for some stacked in the crematorium to give the prisoners the illusion their remains would receive proper burial after the war. However, in November 1944, in an attempt to destroy proof of the enormous number of dead, the ashes of 22,000 victims were thrown in the River Ochre.

A tour of a barracks building used to house prisoners, along with other facilities in the town, was almost as grim as the crematorium. Three-tiered bunks were used in rooms containing 100 to 400 people, with no privacy, no running water or social amenities, and of course an infestation of lice and bed bugs. Food was insufficient and led to diseases killing many.

There is a lot of detail in this memoir of our visit that I will not forget. I think the story is probably very similar to what transpired at the other concentration camps. To be sure, Terezin was primarily a concentration camp, not an extermination facility, but it might as well have been as so many prisoners died of disease, inadequate medical care, and neglect. The story is one of the most incomprehensible and inhumane stories imaginable. Has any fiction writer ever topped the Holocaust for horror and disbelief?

Two other points I thought interesting were that some of the confined people found means to continue to practice their religious beliefs. We were shown a hidden chapel behind the wall in an attic of a residence housing prisoners, and it was considered to be well used.

On June 23, 1944, before the surrender of Germany, a delegation of Nazis including Adolph Eichmann, hosted representatives of the Red Cross for a six-hour visit to the camp. Before this visit, Terezin was dressed up beautifully by the Germans, and the ghetto was renamed a Jewish resettlement area. The Nazi government made an impressive effort of presenting Terezin as a self-administered Jewish settlement in which the inhabitants had the opportunity to survive the war without worry.

The elaborately staged tour culminated with a performance of Verdi's *Requiem* by Terezin's 150-inmate choir. The 90-minute piece speaks of fire and fury, posthumous punishment, and warnings of God's wrath. The conductor had told his choir members: "We will sing to the Nazis what we can't say to them." When the music stopped, the Nazis sat there in silence, but finally nervously applauded.

Our visit to Terezin was unsettling, not to be forgotten. We were both saddened and angered. My prayer on leaving was for all those who died and suffered and for all that we have learned so this does not happen again.

This final day in Prague was not all gloom and doom. After a fine dinner in a riverfront restaurant, we went back to our hotel along the river as a now huge sun set over the Prague Castle in a breathtaking array of pink and gold—a consoling end to a memorable trip.

The Flight to Merida, Venezuela

Sally Parsonson

In June of 2001 Pete and I arrived at Maiquetia, the airport for Caracas, Venezuela, on time and ready to enjoy a pleasant evening in Merida, a city in the Andes mountains near the Venezuelan border with Colombia. But first we had to take a cab to the regional airport where we would board a smaller plane for the short flight to Merida.

At that airport, however, plans changed. The ticket agent at the counter looked carefully through his computer and announced that he had no reservations for us on the flight to Merida. The University of the Andes which had invited Pete to present a short course on traffic management had sent him a letter confirming reservations, so Pete went off to deal with someone in the airline office about the mix-up, while I stood in line with an ever-growing number of passengers. For some reason the agents were not checking anyone in for any flight. Most of the passengers appeared to be in family groups, or perhaps they had just formed families because they had all been waiting together for such a long time.

At one point a young man working behind the counter jumped up on the luggage scales and waved his arms and shouted in Spanish. I gathered from his gestures and from the crowd's reaction that he wanted everyone to line up in two lines. Finally all the passengers managed to do what he wanted and formed two relatively straight lines. He smiled, nodded, and jumped down behind the counter. But the moment he turned his back, the lines disappeared. Everyone jumbled up into their talkative groups again.

I continued to stand where I was waiting for Pete to return with good news about the tickets.

Eventually he did return but said that he had ended up buying new tickets for us since the airline did not seem to be able to locate the ones that the university had told him they reserved and paid for.

Even after Pete returned with confirmed tickets for what was supposed to be an early-afternoon flight, we and all the other prospective passengers continued to stand around and wait.

Then finally something happened. The airline decided to start checking luggage and sending passengers to the gates, but all of those who had been milling around and chatting rushed toward the counter at once so that the young man had to do his shouting-from-the-scales routine again. Once order was restored, Pete and I and the other passengers checked in and were directed to the proper gates.

There, however, we waited again. At least this time we were able to sit down on hard plastic chairs rather than standing in line, but the news was not positive. Pete translated for me the depressing message that the airline was trying to find a pilot. "A *pilot?*" I thought. "Not THE pilot who usually flew this route over the mountains? Someone who knew how to find the airport in Merida?"

At last a competent-looking pilot and two flight attendants showed up. We all boarded the small plane, which took off smoothly. As soon as we were in the air, we could see the sun beginning to set—the end of an afternoon in the most disorganized airport I had ever seen. As the attendant was passing out free drinks, a fruity concoction full of rum, I began to smile. But the pilot made a big announcement which Pete translated with an apologetic smile: "The pilot said that since it's beginning to get dark, we won't be able to land in Merida. There are not adequate lights on the runway there."

"You're kidding" was my response. "Why did they tell us to get on this plane if we can't go there?" Of course, there was no answer to this, so I took a second drink from the flight attendant and resigned myself to our fate, which with a smooth plane ride and a soothing drink, turned out to be not such a bad flight.

However, when we landed in La Vigia, our luck ran out. The airport was tiny and staffed by only one person. There was a large van parked, which was the transport for all of the other passengers from our plane. They were associated with a youth group from the United States and were making a mission trip to assist a small church in the mountains. Everyone piled into the van with their backpacks and luggage and left the two of us standing by the airport office where the manager was waiting to turn off the lights. He had already darkened the runway after our plane left to return to its home base.

Pete discussed our situation with the manager who called a taxi to take us to Merida. Pete said that we would find a hotel and spend the night there. Then we could sort out things tomorrow with our hosts.

Our journey continued on a dark and deserted mountain road. After a few miles we spotted a sign illuminated with bright red lights: "Hotel." But from the highway no building was visible, so down another dark road we went. When we came to the building, our driver said he would check it out. He quickly returned to the car. Pete told me, "It's not our kind of place. The red lights mean something."

So on we went toward the outskirts of Merida. Once we found a suitable hotel, we gathered our luggage and checked in. I only remember falling into bed and sleeping soundly until a phone call woke us up in the morning. Our Merida hosts had located us. They had been at the Merida airport to greet us the night before, and when our plane didn't arrive, they began searching to figure out where we could be.

Fishing

Carolyn Fore

I didn't grow up around fishing and never had any desire to spend my day sitting in a boat waiting for a slimy creature to decide the juicy morsel I had attached to the end of a pole was going to be his next meal. I've been told by many who love the sport (is it a sport?) that there are valid reasons for going fishing, such as the meditative value of sitting on the water for hours without interruption, the excitement of the big catch, the competition of getting the big one, and the story telling about the one that got away.

Hearing my view of fishing will certainly make you wonder why I decided to go on a fly-fishing adventure with my daughter, Amy, one day about ten years ago. Amy heard some friends who were in a volunteer organization she worked with talking about belonging to a ladies' fly-fishing group and how much fun they had. These ladies are closer to my age than hers, so they suggested that she and I join them one day. Since

I knew a couple of them, I let my adventurous daughter convince me that this would be a fun mother-daughter day for us. I even agreed to pay for it since her "just married" budget didn't cover this pricey one-day outing which included lunch, waders, the necessary fishing equipment, a fly-fishing lesson, and a knot-tying class. We were all set for our day on the Chestatee River near Dahlonega, Georgia.

As we drove north on the highway that morning, we discussed our anticipation of this unknown event and the fact that the only people we knew had suddenly had last-minute plan changes and would not be there, so we were completely on our own. I was driving and Amy navigated as we left the main highway, traveled along some back roads, then down a one-lane dirt road, stopping to let a car pass by us in the other direction, making sure neither of us ended up in the bushes. My anticipation, along with anxiety about the day, was growing. As we approached the end of the path, we found a clearing where the cars of those who had arrived before us were parked in front of what appeared to be a horse barn. I was somewhat relieved that there could be civilization here, but I like horses only slightly more than fish, so the sight still wasn't comforting.

We got out of the car and started walking, not sure where to go when Amy pointed out a gorgeous home sitting on the river just to the right of us. It looked like we should head that way. I was starting to feel better.

Maybe there was civilization out here. Arriving at the front of the house, we were greeted by people who escorted us around to the back porch and explained to us that we were allowed to use the porch, the yard, and the access to the river. Then I looked up and was astonished by the spectacular view of the river. We were taken in by the experienced fly fishers, quickly suited up in waders, and told we were ready to give it a try. Due to weather conditions that day the normal schedule would be reversed, meaning we would fish in the morning, having lessons in the water as we fished, then have our knot-tying lessons after lunch on the covered porch.

Getting into the water with an experienced fly fisher at my side, showing me how to hold the fishing rod, how to flick my wrist, and swing the pole around so the lure was way out in the water was fascinating. I finally got the hang of it and was ready to go solo. I could wade around, find a spot I liked, and eventually experienced the thrill of catching a fish—not that whopper you always hear about. It was quite small, and the rules of the day were that all the fish caught would be put back into the water. This was for sport, not for keeps. No problem. After all, what would I do with the fish if I kept it? For me the rushing water over the rapids, the beauty of the surroundings, and the excitement of catching a fish was a thrill.

After a few hours, we were told that it was time for lunch and to go back up to the porch. We got our lunches but needed the inevitable potty break. I looked at the sliding glass doors and asked someone, "Is there a bathroom we can use?" Unfortunately, the answer was, "We aren't allowed in the house, but the outhouse over there is nice." I thought what an oxymoron, *nice* and *outhouse* in the same sentence. But I was desperate. I found it and immediately noticed that the wood was new, not some old outhouse that had been sitting there for years. While it did not have running water or a flushing toilet, it did have a mirror, hand lotion, nice towels, and as many of the niceties of a ladies' restroom as you could put in an outhouse. I went back to the porch and told my daughter to give it a try; it was nice. She glared at me and said "you've got to be kidding," but went for it. When she came back, she laughed and told me it was the best outhouse she had ever seen, but she wasn't willing to say it was nice. After all, it was still an outhouse.

The afternoon agenda would be as promised, to learn to tie lures with different knots. The instructors were handing out the materials when several people from Atlanta got up and said they were leaving because they were all going to a big wedding that afternoon. Amy leaned over and whispered to me, "Wouldn't it be a lot more fun to tour a couple of the wineries while we're up here?" I sort of nodded at her and started packing up my stuff. The instructor looked at us and said, "Oh, do you two have to leave, too?" Amy quickly said, "Yes, this has been so much fun! Thank you!" and off we went.

That afternoon we visited Three Sisters Winery and one other and had an afternoon that was much more to our liking. I think I'm glad I tried fly fishing, but I don't plan to do it again. Visiting wineries is much more my style, and I'm certain my daughter feels the same way.

A Week in Merida, Venezuela

Sally Parsonson

After the upsets of the flight to Merida and the discovery that both the lush tropical hotel where we spent the first night and the apartment which had been loaned to us were heavily guarded by watchmen with guns, I tried to enjoy the beautiful city in the mountains. But every experience there seemed to include unsettling moments.

Merida's prime tourist attraction, the *teleferico*, was the highest and longest cable car in the world, IF it was working. That day it was, although later I wasn't so sure I was. Going up Pico Espejo seemed a good way to spend a peaceful Sunday. We headed up away from the warmth and green trees of Merida to the first stop, where some of our fellow riders, appropriately dressed in hiking boots and shorts, disembarked. They began a trek across the *paramo*, the high, treeless plateau in tropical South America that would be called a moor in England. Pete and I, unprepared to hike, disembarked to read the information boards near the exit. We learned about the indigenous birds, animals, and vegetation of the area. I was especially interested in *frailejón*, a rare flowering plant with yellow daisy-like flowers, unique to the *paramo*. It bloomed in this season, and seeing the expanse of fields covered with flowers was a highlight of the day.

But then, as we took the next cable car up, I began to feel chilly. I had worn summer clothes. After all it was June, in a tropical country well south of Atlanta. But the thought of the season didn't keep me from shivering. We elected not to exit at the next station and stayed within the comparative warmth of the cable car. At the third station we had to switch to a smaller but more enclosed type of car, and, as we transferred to it, we felt the effects of the high altitude as well as the cold. Yes, I had read the signs at the station entrance in Merida, the last station was almost 4800 meters high. Of course I hadn't converted that to feet, so I didn't realize that the summit was 15,630 feet high. Fortunately the last stop had both heating and altitude-adapting stations, which we took advantage of until we could catch the next car down.

The next day Pete began teaching his two-week course in traffic engineering. Many of the students were in residence at the University of Merida, but others, including some who were graduates working in the field, came from all over the Republic. One day when Pete was teaching, I joined the group for a coffee break with the students. Pete asked a girl from Caracas how life was in the city where he had once worked and lived. She began by saying that she was happy to be enjoying the peaceful atmosphere in Merida. Of course I listened closely to her words. "Peaceful?" I thought. "This place? With all the guards and guns?"

The student went on to relate a recent experience in Caracas: "I was driving alone to take photographs of a recent project when I stopped for a traffic light in the middle of the city," she said. "Something alerted me to look to my left. A man was standing by my car pointing a gun at me with one hand, and with his other hand he was gesturing toward my camera on the front seat. As I glanced toward the camera, I noticed another man on the right side of the car also with a gun pointed at me and my camera." She paused. "I didn't wait for the light to turn green." As she finished her tale, all the traffic engineers at the table began to discuss the dangerous situations in Venezuela, but, since everyone was speaking in Spanish, I tuned out, happy for once that I didn't understand every word.

Saturday was my final day in Merida, and, although Pete would stay on to teach for a second week, I was comforted to think of returning to our Sandy Springs home where guns were not so much a topic of conversation. We hired a guide with a car to take us to one more tourist site: a stone-and-coral chapel constructed by a native artist on the mountain road leading through the Andes to Colombia. We drove up and up and round and round to reach the chapel, but with the location covered in snow and ice and us in summer clothes, our visit was brief.

As we headed back down to Merida, there was one final stop: a highly-recommended country restaurant for lunch. With our guide we were seated on an open porch at the back of the rustic building overlooking a pastoral scene of low green mountains dotted with a few farmhouses and grazing horses and cattle. The restaurant thoughtfully provided woolen blankets in case visitors, like us, had arrived in summer clothing. Yes, we needed them. At last I was both peaceful and warm in Merida.

But then, suddenly, gunshots erupted. The sudden noise seemed quite close to us. I ducked under the blanket and under the table. Was this the Wild West? But the guide spoke quickly, "Don't worry. I forgot. Today is St. John's Day. We always celebrate with guns. It's tradition." As I came out from under the blanket and tried to breathe, I saw gray puffs of smoke from gunshots all over the valley. The action was nearby: horsemen, who were riding like cowboys with six-shooters through the open fields. Later that day, we heard and saw the city's holiday fireworks for the saint's day from the safety of the Merida apartment, but with all the sudden noises I had doubts that I would breathe freely until I was safely home in Atlanta.

Although the flight to Merida had not been what I expected, the next day's return flight made me question which of the two was the worst. As soon as the plane lifted off the runway, my head felt as if it might explode: a sinus infection, I realized, perhaps from the altitude and the cold excursion to the mountains the day before. And, as I waited at the Caracas airport for the flight to Atlanta, I huddled under my jacket in pain and tried to ignore the pairs of military guards, armed as usual with their "street-sweepers," who paced back and forth in the terminal.

On the Atlanta flight I pulled the airline blanket over me and tried to sleep, gathering strength to drive home from the airport. But one more hazard awaited me. When I pulled into our driveway, I suddenly halted. The trunk of an oak tree, knocked down by a storm, completely blocked my way. I locked the car, dragged my suitcase inside, and remembered Scarlett O'Hara's words: "After all, tomorrow is another day."

ONE RED ROSE AND A WHITE CARNATION

Janet Wilson

January 27, 1923...the date is handwritten on a tiny piece of paper glued inside the cover of a tiny faded-blue box that Grandma gave me. I smile as I read Grandma's words...

"In this box is a rose and a carnation that we gave to one another on the night of our engagement, my Beloved and me, Mr. Louis Amato and Anna Di Paola, with all our love."

The beginning.

At the turn of the century, on the 27th of November in 1899, an infant boy was born in Calabria to Guessipi Amato and Rose Michelli Amato. Following a terrible earthquake, as the story was told to me, the boy was found nestled in his mother's arms where she lay dead under a door jamb in the building where they were living. Not long after that, in 1904, the boy's dad, the aunt who would soon become the boy's mother, and the rest of the Amato family left Italy. The boy would live his childhood years in the little mountain town of Revelstoke, British Columbia.

Meanwhile, in the little mountain town of Giungano, near Salerno, Italy, an infant girl was born to Francesco Di Paolo and Severia Cantalupo Di Paolo. In 1903, the little girl's father decided to emigrate to America. The little girl's mother was denied passage; she was pregnant with her fifth child. Leaving his wife and daughter behind, the father and the three older children departed from the port of Naples and arrived in New York Harbor seven to ten days later. The girl would grow up in Harlem.

How very grateful I am that these two children were eventually to meet and become my maternal grandparents. No one could have loved me more than my grandparents, Louis and Anna Amato. Grandpa was not tall in stature, perhaps five foot seven. He had wavy dark black hair that gradually turned salt-and-pepper gray. By then he had a round bald spot not quite the size of the yarmulke worn by the owner of the grocery store, one floor below on street level at 2363 Valentine Avenue. Grandpa had a strong work ethic. He was honorable and trustworthy. He was always impeccably dressed and well groomed. Grandpa took pride in his work for the New York Central Railroad as head agent at the Yonkers Freight Yard, but he was especially proud of his two daughters, Rose and Sadie, and later, six grandchildren of which I was the first-born.

Grandma had a creamy porcelain complexion and big brown eyes that always seemed to be gleaming with mischief. She was but five feet in height, a bit round, and full-bodied. On the left side of her bottom lip there was an enlarged purple area, perhaps a lingering reminder of her having suffered sleeping sickness which necessitated that she be sent to the country for three months for proper rest. Her first-born child, my mom, was not yet a year old at the time. Grandma had black hair until she was in her eighties when she suddenly decided to let it go completely gray. I wonder if it had anything to do with the loss of Grandpa; they had been married fifty-five years.

My grandma was a bit of a clown. She kept everyone laughing, while Grandpa was the more serious one. I remember times when we visited for Sunday dinners and I would help pinch off the ends of the string beans she was going to cook. While the rest of the family was in the living room, she would encourage me to play her little game of dropping some of the bean tips out the window over passers-by. Oh, what fun this was for her... to be just a little mischievous. There was another game she played as people walked by one floor below her kitchen window. After using the dustmop on the floors throughout her apartment, Grandma would stand back and away from that window, extend the mop handle so the mop was just outside the window, and give it a good shake. We would quickly glance downward to catch the look on the faces of her victims as the dust bunnies flurried and just as quickly step back from the window and giggle.

Grandma was not always so jolly. She had had an unhappy childhood. She was only seven years old when her mother died and her father returned to Italy to marry his wife's younger sister. The two then came back to this country. Grandma told me terrible stories of how she was treated by her stepmother. According to Grandma, this woman made her feel unwanted and like she was nothing but a bad girl. Grandma had three older brothers, two younger half-brothers, and then a younger half-sister. The other children were invited to the dinner table, but not Grandma. She was the classic Cinderella, made to do the chores and then eat the scraps. The other children soon learned it was easy to blame Anna for all of their wrongdoing. One day someone showed up at their apartment door wanting to know why Anna had not been at school. Her stepmother refused to open the door. Later that evening she was so angry at Grandma that she grabbed the child's only doll right from her arms and threw it out the window. Grandma was not to have her doll... neither would she be schooled beyond the third grade.

During the daytime while her stepmother was out, Grandma was left alone in the apartment. The refrigerator was always padlocked, so Grandma could not eat or drink anything except water and, if she was lucky, a cracker or two. Maybe that's why Grandma loved food, glorious food. From my earliest memory, Grandma ravaged her plate at meals. She was always the first to be finished and first to help herself to seconds with a smile.

I looked forward to Grandma and Grandpa's visits to Yorktown Heights where my family and I lived after moving from Davidson Avenue in the Bronx the month of my seventh birthday. They always, every time, arrived with boxes of Chiclets, Hershey chocolate bars, Jewish marble pound cake, and my favorite, chocolate cream pie.

Whenever I had the opportunity, I spent time with my grandparents. They liked having me around as much as I liked being with them. I loved riding the train...the New York Central Railroad from Croton-Harmon station to University Heights. From there we either took a taxi or, if Grandma wasn't with us, Grandpa and I would walk to 2363 Valentine Avenue.

Grandpa loved to take me on errands. Just downstairs and around the corner was the little family-run market. We chatted with Mr. Mandel, the owner, while we picked fresh fruits and vegetables, and grabbed the milk and bread we needed. One day I met his daughter, Lois, and we became friends. We played nok-hockey and handball at the corner park near Ryer Avenue. Sometimes we played stickball in the street. I still remember proudly roofing the ball. Grandpa also took me to the Chinese laundry where we dropped off suits to be dry-cleaned and picked up the already-laundered shirts neatly wrapped in brown paper packages. Then there was the pharmacy where we got Grandma's medications. A box of Ex-lax was always on the list to be purchased. One of my favorite errands to go on was to the bagel basement. I was fascinated as we went below ground to where those scrumptious round bread treats were baked and sold still warm from the oven. Pumpernickel, sesame seed, garlic, onion...umm!

Grandma loved to take me shopping. Before leaving the apartment she took her shower, then left the bathroom door ajar and called out to me, "It's so steamy in here I'm going to leave the door open, so please stay in the kitchen." I was already busy folding sheets of Grandpa's New York Central Railroad paper to add to my growing fleet of paper boats lining up on the kitchen table. Or I was writing a letter home to my parents and sisters, Diane and Gail. At times, I was using my crayons or colored pencils to color all the flower designs on a silky white paper napkin, making it a beautiful work of art. If the little brown radio on the shelf above my head was on, I was singing along with the Everly Brothers, Connie Francis, Frankie Avalon, Elvis, or the Beach Boys. When Grandma was finally ready, we left the apartment and headed for Alexander's on

Fordham Road, not far from St. James Park. Everyone else in the city seemed to have the same idea. We all stood outside the main doors until 9:00 a.m. Suddenly, as the doors opened, there was chaos...people pushing and shoving to find the best bargains of the day. I remember watching two ladies pulling at the same handbag. Their faces turned angry and their bodies tensed, neither wanting to give the item up. One finally did let go. The other, left holding the handbag she was determined to have, looked it over once more, tossed it back onto the display table, and walked away. She must not have wanted it after all. Shopping with Grandma was almost always an adventure. Harriet the Spy would have loved it. Once Grandma found what she wanted to buy, we would go to the cashier. After the purchase was rung up on the register and the items were bagged, the cashier would give Grandma the gift boxes she was entitled to receive. If the girl gave her one gift box and she felt she was entitled to three, there was no way we would leave the store without getting those two extra boxes.

After leaving Alexander's with new things for me and something to bring home to my sisters, too, Grandma took me to Krums, a well-known candy and ice cream shop on the Grand Concourse. Grandma let me order anything I wanted, which was almost always an all-chocolate hot-fudge sundae. She let me think she was there for me, but I knew she wanted her pineapple sundae. Grandma loved pineapple sundaes. Before leaving Krums, we would buy a box of butter crunch to take back to Grandpa.

Every summer I got to spend a week or two at Grandma and Grandpa's. Grandpa loved to walk. He loved music and people. He loved to take me to Poe Park to feed the pigeons. There was usually a performance going on at the gazebo. All around it people talked, sang, and danced. Some just smiled, and others closed their eyes and listened. Still others seemed to ignore everything around them and continued reading their copy of the *Daily News* or *Mirror*. There were children to play with and dogs to pet. Grandpa loved to go most when there was an orchestra playing, but he also liked the nights of square dancing and magic performances.

Nearly a century since the engagement of one young man and one young woman...

It is Autumn, my favorite season of the year. I love the changing color of the landscape and the crispness of the air, especially on vividly-blue-sky days. I love feeling soft winds brushing against my face and watching summer's leaves dance from the trees. Sipping cider and eating sugar-coated donuts still warm from the press makes an apple-picking day complete. October is a perfect month to be born; my birthday is October 8th. Christopher Columbus was born on October 12th. Columbus Day is a national holiday, though nowadays many find this a questionable observance. I understand why having read Jane Yolen's picture book, *Encounter*, to my third-grade students. Yet, the date itself will always remain special to me. October 12th marks the anniversary of the two people who shaped my life, two people I loved dearly, two people who gave each other one red rose and a white carnation upon their engagement... my maternal grandparents, Louis and Anna Amato.

Happy Anniversary, Grandma and Grandpa!

PART FIVE

Yes, ...There Is a Santa Claus!

Stefan Fatzinger

D o you remember when you were told there is no
Santa Claus? I do; it was one of the most traumatic
days of my life. In hindsight, however, as a person who
always looks for the proverbial "silver lining," it was also
an event that has led to my love of Christmas.

No matter how hard I churn the water of my
memories, I only remember one Christmas as a child.
That is because God provided my mind with a "delete"
tab that has allowed me to selectively wipe out most
of my unpleasant memories, particularly those from
my childhood. It was not until I began having my own
children that the enchantment of family Christmas
holidays again became part of my life's internal photo
album. But one Christmas was magical and perfect. I
was five. On Christmas Eve, my mother, father, brother,
and I went to the Moravian church in Bethlehem,
Pennsylvania. With the lights dimmed and candles
burning, the wondrous voice of my father singing O

Holy Night as a solo filled the small sanctuary. The memory still gives me chills, raises the hair on my neck, and brings moisture to my eyes. And then as the service is ending, with the lights still dimmed and the candles burning, the sanctuary is again filled with my father's voice singing the first verse of *Silent Night*, first in German and then English, before the congregation joins in to sing the final five verses. After arriving home, my brother and I become delirious with glee as we discover that the gifts are already under our Christmas tree. Santa Claus has arrived! After being allowed to open one gift before going to bed, we fall happily asleep anticipating Christmas morning. Oh, what a wonderful day!

But that was my last family Christmas until I became an adult. The following year my brother and I were in a foster home; then we spent several years in an orphanage, followed by more years of a living nightmare.

The spring after that magical Christmas, I had my first heart-to-heart conversation with my father. Dad informed me that there was no Santa Claus. I was at first devastated; I did not want to accept this news, and I still don't these many years later. I therefore rejected my father for the first time, but not the last. I needed to believe in a being who brought joy and happiness into people's lives, particularly as events were to unfold for my brother and me. It became necessary for me to believe in the goodness, kindness, delight, merriment, and cheer that Kris Kringle breathes into life. So, like the boy in *The Polar Express*, I have always been able to hear the bell. I believe. And to ensure that belief, I have in my later years, become Santa Claus.

I discovered about twenty years ago that not only is my hair white, but so is my beard. In addition to being the "jolly old elf," during the entire year BC (Before COVID), I teach English to immigrants, tutor 4th grade Hispanic students, sleep with the homeless, feed the hungry, visit congressmen and senators to battle the sexual exploitation of children, and provide pastoral care for my congregation. Then beginning on October 1st I stop shaving and grow a pure white beard for the upcoming Christmas season. I began doing this for my 4th grade Mexican students who, prior to COVID, I tutored every Tuesday and Thursday. I have continued this tradition for all my friends, family, and students ever since. Once I also was able to transform myself into Santa Claus for approximately 65 children ages two to ten at the Optimist Club's party in Sandy Springs, Georgia. How can I explain the joy and wonderment of the children who all believe in me as they hug, smile, laugh, and sit on my lap while their parents' phones are snapping our picture when they receive their two gifts from me? Their love, anticipation, happiness, and true belief fill my heart and my soul.

It all begins, however, on December 1st when I put on my Santa Claus cloak, fill a sack with Advent calendars that have 24 doors numbered 1-24 behind each of which is a piece of chocolate, and pass them out to the 4th grade students while relating to them the Christmas traditions in Germany. They love it, but it is I who derive the most joy and love as I see the happiness on their faces and in their eyes. Yes, Mia, Angela, Mitzy, Carlos, and all, there is a Santa Claus!

December 2020 would be somewhat different since I was not able to provide my students with their Advent calendars that year. But I have heard that when a door is closed, another is opened and that is what occurred. During a Zoom meeting with my ESL students, I discovered that an 8-year-old daughter of one of the students wanted a Maileg dollhouse for Christmas. But her mother could not afford it. The perfect opportunity was thus presented for Santa, and, after consultation with the elves, a Maileg dollhouse was on its way to one 8-year-old young lady!

While overseas for twenty-one years, I also discovered that the Christmas season is a unique time of year all over the world. During my fourteen years in Germany, I visited Christmas markets every weekend during Advent, observing the rosy cheeks, smiles, and laughter of children and adults while we ate bratwurst and drank gluhwein in falling snow. In Korea and Japan, I marveled at the Christmas celebrations and decorations in non-traditional Christian countries. I have spent a Christmas with three of my children in

Disneyland Paris where we stood in the frigid cold waiting on the rides, enjoying every minute, as did all the other park visitors. I have observed the Chamorros on Guam wrapping themselves in Christmas lights following a devastating super typhoon that destroyed the island but not the Christmas spirit of the islanders.

For a little over a month, people the world over, myself included, stop long enough to give more of themselves. Smiles replace snarls; happiness replaces sadness; families and friends gather; laughter fills the air. It is a time for reconciliation, and a time when people speak of hope, peace, joy, and goodwill for all mankind. Finally, it is a celebration of birth and renewal, but also of love, the love of man and God. I believe!

THE NIGHT SHELTER AT ALL SAINTS'

Sally Parsonson

In January of 1984 I went with Holy Innocents' volunteers to staff the night shelter at All Saints' Episcopal Church. This experience with the homeless was outside my comfort zone. All the previous volunteers had remarked first on the smell. "Massive toe jam" described it, but those who had already been to the shelter had warned us, "It's not so bad if you stay in the hall, but if you stay a while in the volunteer room or go down to the restroom, the shock of re-entry is almost unbearable."

Visual impressions were more varied. Most were black men, not too young or too old. However, a few appeared quite old. One white man looked especially "grandfatherly" in a white shirt with a pointed, out-of-style collar. His beige vest drooped over his big belly. One black man looked the part of a street person. If I had been a costume designer for a movie, I would have dressed a street character like him: blue jeans, long blue-denim jacket under which he wore a very dirty white shirt jacket with black sleeves. He had the requisite knitted cap, or rather two caps, a dark red one topped by a brown one. From the back he looked young, but his face was old and lined, partially covered with a full but scrawny brown beard.

Two women, both square-faced, with straight greasy-looking short hair, seemed to fit into the group. One said she'd had a hysterectomy two months ago. "Cancer," she said. The two of them were worried about one of the young black men, who they said had tried to get into their room a couple of nights ago. Apparently he had given one of them a ticket to enter the shelter that night and expected "repayment."

Then there was an older white man, whom I heard someone call "Charlie." He was wearing a pair of tan plaid polyester slacks that appeared to me to be identical to the slacks I had crafted on my sewing machine in the spirit of the "do-it-yourself 1970s" for my then-husband Guy. Charlie slept as closely as possible to the door, apparently a favored place, because of relative safety. He wanted us to keep safe for him a paper bag from The Varsity containing his tobacco pouch and lighter.

Another man asked us to keep his bag with "all his earthly possessions," as Anne Shirley in *Anne of Green Gables* described her carpetbag. I think this man was the one who most closely resembled in appearance what I had thought of as a typical street person. But most of the group was atypical.

A plumpish blond boy walked, or rather "swished," by. He had lovely clean blond hair, shoulder-length, but a terribly scarred or pock-marked face. The record for "swishing," however, belonged to a black man with a page-boy wig. That man came by every few minutes, just trying, it seemed, to show off for us.

The parade to the bathrooms was endless, a constant traffic pattern. About 10 o'clock, a man named Larry asked to be let out. He wanted, he said, to go home to Mama. She'd feed him, he thought, because he wasn't drunk tonight.

"Demon Drink" is the curse here. One tattooed man named Bob described his day for us. He'd left All Saints' and gone to the Krystal, but it wasn't open (perhaps because of the snow?), so he had gone on to The Varsity, but it wasn't open either. So all that was left for him was to buy a bottle of wine to stave off boredom. He didn't account for his whereabouts after he bought the wine. Maybe he made it last all day. He told us he'd been in 'Nam, and had been in the Navy for twelve years before he got discharged. "Honorably," he noted. Also he had been a subcontractor in painting, drywall, and sheetrock. He was good at his work, and now, he continued, he was getting his life back together with the help of Christ. He wore a small silver cross that he told us had been a Christmas present. Although he said he'd never sell it, I imagine he might if he wanted a drink badly enough. It appeared to be cheap metal, not worth the price of a bottle. Bob bemoaned how badly people treated each other these days. I kept listening as he told about helping a man outside the Krystal on Ponce de Leon. The man was having an epileptic seizure, so Bob put a comb in his mouth to prevent the man from biting himself. Then he said he " 'lowed as how" he hoped no one would have a seizure at the shelter tonight. I of course agreed.

A man named Ananias, which he told us was a name from the fifth chapter of Acts, talked to our little group for a long time. He said he came from a little town 30 miles outside of Houston. He first came to Atlanta in 1974 for a job transfer, but he soon had to leave the job because his mother died. It costs $108.52 to get back to Houston, he said, and he doesn't have that much. He would like to see his father since his father has had three heart attacks, the last one in November, but he still doesn't have the money, he said with a sniff.

One of the last men to enter the shelter was a young white man with black hair, a thin but rather nice face. He didn't seem at all dressed for life on the street. We looked around to see if we could find him some more suitable clothes, but all we could find were some hats in the volunteer room. We planned to give him one before he left in the morning.

Once I became used to the smell, the shelter was a nicer place to be than I had expected. No crisis occurred. We did not have to use the police or fire department telephone numbers that night. Most of our visitors said "thank you" for the two cold sandwiches and tea that we gave them for breakfast. After we herded everyone out, I drove home to my clean, warm bed with tears in my eyes.

Dixie

Jeannie Longley

This is the story of Dixie, a hamster that showed me the presence of God's love in many ways. It may seem ludicrous that a *hamster*, of all creatures, could do this, but the reader may decide for him/herself.

I must admit that before we had Dixie, I wasn't too fond of hamsters. Our previous experience as a family was limited to two vengeful and biting little rodents named Cinnamon and Santa, who'd mercifully died a few years earlier, having seemingly outlived the normal lifespan of hamsters. Ever since they had died, my daughter Dori had been pestering me for another hamster. After she produced a two-page, single-spaced, typed essay about why we should get another hamster, I finally conceded. We have friends who were desperately trying to find homes for a new litter of baby hamsters, and, as they had graciously taken one of Cinnamon and Santa's offspring in the past, I felt obligated. Hence Dixie arrived at the Longley household.

Now I have to say, Dixie was a *great* hamster. We all
adored her. She would cuddle right up into the crook
of my arm and snuggle peacefully. She would wrinkle
her little nose at Christy and Tracy, our two Bichon
doggies, who were fascinated with her. We would place
her in her little plastic exercise sphere on the floor, and
she would scamper about with the dogs right on her
tail. She was as curious about the dogs as they were
about her, and she was fearless. She was wonderful,
and she was part of the family.

One Friday morning, when Dori was in fifth grade, she
came down for breakfast and discovered to her horror
that Dixie was not in her cage. The door on the top
was ajar, but Dori insisted she had closed it the night
before. We looked all over, but there was no sign of the
hamster. Dori was beside herself, sobbing with anguish.
Her brother Cliff, a ninth grader, went on to school, but
Dori was in no condition to go. Finally, around ten in
the morning, she had calmed down enough to head to
class. I promised her that I would stop and pick up a
Havaheart trap on my way home.

The timing could not have been worse. Dori was
scheduled to take the SSAT the next morning, which
would be a big factor in determining where she would
be in school the next year. I worried that she would be
in no shape to take the test.

After school that day, Dori's friend Caroline came
over, and the two of them looked all over the house

for Dixie. My fear was that one of the dogs might have eaten her, but I decided to keep that to myself.

The two girls devised a plan to determine where Dixie was hiding. They decided that she must be on the first floor, where her cage was located. In each room, they placed two jar lids, one with two pieces of hamster kibble, the other with a little water. They then closed the door to each room and blocked the threshold with a towel. In addition, they put our two hamster wheels in two of the rooms, in hopes of enticing Dixie out of her hiding spot. Their plan was to reassess the food situation the next day. Their ingenuity was admirable.

I tried to soothe Dori as much as possible, so that she would be able to rest well before the test, but I was anxious about how her test-taking ability would be impacted. That evening, Lester and Cliff, my husband and son, joined in the search. None of us wanted to acknowledge the likelihood that we would not see Dixie again.

I finally got Dori settled in bed, and amazingly she drifted off to sleep easily. A few hours later Cliff was playing a video game in the basement, and he heard a squeaking noise coming from above. He soon realized that it was from the hamster wheel in the room over his head. He dashed up the stairs, threw open the door and switched on the light just in time to see Dixie dart behind a bookcase full of heavy textbooks. He called his father, and the two of them managed to move the bookcase and with a swift movement capture the hamster. We were elated.

At Cliff's request, I awakened him early the next morning so that he could wake Dori and present her with her hamster. He was so happy to do it, and of course she was delighted beyond measure. I marveled at a brother and sister's love for one another.

There is one footnote to this story. I was secretly convinced that Dori had left the cage open. A few weeks later we were out of town and my nephew Andy was house- and dog-sitting. He was in the family room one evening, watching television, and heard a noise. He looked over, just in time to see that Dixie had popped the door to her cage open and was about to escape. After that, we covered it with a weight. I should never have doubted Dori's word. She is as honest as the day is long.

One evening a year or so later, Dori, then twelve, came to me with concern in her voice. She was worried that Dixie wasn't acting herself. We took a close look at her. In retrospect, I recalled that she had indeed been a little lethargic for a day or so and hadn't been eating much. On close inspection we found a blackened area just beneath her jaw. I feared the worst—a cancer of some sort. The first thing the next morning I called our veterinarian's office.

Unfortunately, the only veterinarian in the practice who saw small animals was out of the office and couldn't see Dixie for a week. I knew that our pet would die before then without intervention. I checked Dixie who was still quiet in her cage, looking weak. I got out the telephone book, and started going through the Yellow Pages, calling one veterinarian after another in our neighborhood. I found one who could see her in four days and made an appointment. I kept calling, and each time when I got an earlier appointment, I cancelled the one I had made previously. Then I saw the ad—"All Creatures Animal Hospital." I had passed it over earlier, as it was far away. But then I noticed the small print: "specializing in small animals." I knew this was the place. Now granted, by this point it was Friday afternoon, and Dixie had never been a patient in the practice, but I made the call. The receptionist was as pleasant as she could be and gave us an appointment for the next afternoon.

Dixie seemed about the same the next morning but wasn't any worse. At the appointed time, we headed up Mount Vernon Highway to Dunwoody. We arrived at "All Creatures," and the place was a zoo (no pun intended!). It was literally crawling with creatures of every size and sort. We were greeted warmly by the staff and filled out the necessary paperwork. As we waited anxiously, a large, caged bird was delivered from the back office to a family waiting next to us. They were delighted when they saw their bird and commented on what a dramatic improvement there had been and that the bird was just

like its old self. Upon hearing this, of course, our hopes
soared.

Eventually it was our turn, and we were taken
back with Dixie to the examination room, where the
attendant took a brief history and weighed Dixie. After
a short wait, the veterinarian entered. As I mentioned
before, the waiting room was chaotic, and I knew that
the vet must feel harried. But we would never have
known it from her dealings with us. She made us feel
as if our concerns were the only thing on her mind and
that she had all the time in the world. She examined
Dixie gently, spoke with us, and then laid our options
out on the table. Dixie was gravely ill due to an abscess
in her lower jaw. Secondary to this, she was weak and
dehydrated from lack of appetite. Without intervention,
the vet thought that Dixie would die in a day or two.
Taking Dixie home to her own surroundings was one of
the choices we were given. The other two choices were
to euthanize her or to start subcutaneous fluids and
antibiotics, and to operate as soon as Dixie was stable
in order to drain the abscess. Even with aggressive
treatment, the vet voiced doubt that Dixie would pull
through.

The vet said she would give us some time to decide
what to do, but made it clear the decision was up to
us. I must admit that my first question was "What is
this going to cost?" Aggressive treatment would be fifty
dollars, including the surgery. The vet stepped out to

allow us to confer in privacy. At Holy Innocents' we were in the middle of Project Starfish, a church outreach to benefit our sister parish in St. Matthieu, Haiti, and all I could think of was of all the good those dollars could accomplish in Haiti. I thought to myself, "I mean, we're talking about a hamster, for God's sake!" But one look at my daughter's face gave me the answer. We would try to save Dixie.

The vet returned to the room, and we gave her our decision. By this time, it was close to five in the afternoon. We were told that fluids and antibiotics would be started right away, and the surgery would be after that, or first thing Sunday morning. We gave Dixie a little hug, and headed home, anxious, but feeling more at ease.

That night we had a few families over to celebrate the birthday of a close friend. At nine-thirty as we were serving coffee and dessert, the telephone rang. It was the vet. They had done everything they could, but Dixie hadn't survived the surgery. I think we all had had the time mentally to prepare for this, but it was still tough news. As it started to sink in, I had the thought that here it was, nine-thirty on a Saturday night, and this woman I didn't know was still at work, trying to save the life of a little hamster just because she understood what it meant to our family. I was in awe. We were told that the animal hospital could dispose of the body, or we could retrieve it. I said I would let them know first thing in the morning.

Half-afraid that the body would already be gone, I called the office after church Sunday morning. But no, the receptionist informed me, it was there, and I could come any time that day. I went by myself to get the body, as I thought it might be too upsetting to Dori. In marked contrast to the day before, the waiting room was empty, and a different receptionist was at the desk, also as pleasant as could be. She was wearing a brightly colored shift, and her head was covered with a colorful turban. I was a little embarrassed to be there retrieving the body of a hamster and didn't exactly know what to say, but, as soon as I said my name, she said, "Oh, you must be here for Dixie. Let me get her."

She went to the back and reappeared a minute later carrying a small white box gingerly on her outstretched palms. On the top of the box in embellished letters, it said, "Dixie." There was a little flourish underneath the name, and the "i" was dotted with a small heart. She came around the corner and presented it to me. I burst into tears. Now, mind you, I can count on one hand the number of times I have cried at a movie. Ask my kids; I'm just not a real crier. Needless to say, I was absolutely mortified! The receptionist gave me a hug, and led me around to a bench to sit, with an offer for some cold water. I insisted that I was fine and couldn't believe I was making such a fuss over a hamster. "Honey," she said, "that's not just a little hamster. It was part of your family, and you've lost it. That hamster was part of you, and your daughter. It brought a lot of joy to you, and it's natural for you to be sad. Just imagine if you weren't sad at all. Believe me, I know just what you're going through. I lost a son in November."

I was dumbfounded. My jaw dropped open, but I was literally speechless. "Oh, My God!" I finally managed to say, "How do you manage to get out of bed in the morning?"

"Honey, that's just what I do," she replied, her eyes misting. "I get out of the bed in the morning, put one foot in front of the other, and keep on going. Before I know it, it's time to get back in the bed."

I sat for a few minutes longer, collected Dixie, and myself, and headed home. It was a beautiful spring day. When I got home, Dori and her best buddy were waiting for me. We didn't open the box. We went to the back yard, dug a hole underneath the dogwood tree, and had a little memorial service. We adorned the grave with a little stick cross we lashed together and the flowers from dinner the night before. Over the ensuing months, the flowers gradually decomposed, and even the little cross eventually broke up.

What remains clear is the memory of that little hamster, the joy that she brought my daughter and our family, the selfless and loving care that we were shown by strangers, the realization that everyone has a story, and the courage demonstrated by everyday people, every day.

A Stitch in Time

Jeannie Longley

I have always admired those who could recite poetry or quote a Bible verse or an author from memory. I'm not one of those folks. In fact, sometimes after hearing what I consider to be a moving sermon, I find myself struggling to recall the content just a day or two later. But during one of my first visits to Holy Innocents' back in 1993, one of the priests made a comment during a sermon that has stayed with me. I don't recall the exact words, but the gist was that one would get out of one's church community and spiritual life what one put into it.

At that point in my life, with a busy career and two small children, I felt like I had a lot on my plate. I knew I wasn't getting a lot out of my church or spiritual life. Although it didn't seem like an intentional decision at that time, I decided to "say yes" a year or two later to one of the requests in the church bulletin, and I became a Sunday school teacher.

Since that time, I've responded to many requests in those Sunday bulletins and have had the opportunity to serve in a multitude of ways. One of those requests was for stitchers to work on needlepoint kneelers, designed specifically for our sanctuary and given very generously by parishioners at Holy Innocents'.

I have always loved needlepoint and had had a little experience doing it. I made an eyeglass case during my college years and loved it until my pocketbook got yanked off of my shoulder. It was the item I missed most in that purse. Although I'd made a couple of pillows over the years, I had not done any needlepoint since the early 1980s. So, when the request for stitchers came out, I ignored it for several months, and it went away. But I thought about how much I loved the needlepoint kneelers in my childhood parish, so when the request reappeared, I thought about it again, and eventually said "yes."

When I picked up my canvas and yarn from the church office in July 2014, I have to admit that I was overwhelmed. Compared with the projects I had done in the past, this one was gargantuan! I had never worked in a frame, and the type of stitch, the basketweave stitch, was also one with which I was not familiar. One would think that as a retired gynecologist, it would not have been a struggle to learn, but I'm handicapped by being both left-handed and not very spatially gifted. Getting those first little rectangles completed was a challenge. The phrase, "What was I thinking?" was on autorepeat in my mind each time I sat down. But the design on my canvas is gorgeous. It is a representation of a floral print by Thomas Ventulett, the architect for our new church space, and I was inspired to stay with the project.

In August 2014, when we stitchers were asked to bring our canvases to the Sunday service in order to have them blessed, I was so ashamed of how little I had done that I didn't remove it from the case I was using to store it. I made a point of coming to the stitchers' gatherings when I could and always did some work beforehand so I wouldn't feel totally humiliated. But between meetings the canvas was often out of sight and out of mind.

I finally decided to put a calendar in with my canvas, and to check off each time I stitched, even if it was only for a short while. There were a lot of blank days for many months, but somehow I made the decision to be proactive and just stitch! I have grown to love this time. Sometimes I will listen to a podcast of talk-show hosts Diane Rehm or Terry Gross or to music, but many times I just sit quietly. I have found the same peace I find on a long solo run, and I have come to recognize it as a form of prayer.

This year, for Lenten disciplines, I decided to add on instead of giving something up. In past years, I had given up either dessert, chocolate, coffee, or alcohol, and none of those were good fits. I decided to read the daily lectionary and to stitch each day during the Lenten season, and, although I wasn't perfect, it ended up being very fulfilling. And I am trying to follow the Reverend Lisa Zaina's admonition from the Easter issue of *Anam Cara*: "Don't put Jesus back on the cross by heaving a sigh of relief that Lent is done and going back to your pre-Lenten self."

Although I still have a long way to go with my canvas, I already know that I'm going to miss it when it's completed. I'm grateful to those who had the vision for this project, and I look forward to receiving Communion on the kneelers.

CHRISTMAS SINGS

Janet Wilson

I t is December 23rd of the year of Covid-19, just two
days before Christmas. Christmas has always filled
my heart with joy, but this year I am feeling a sadness at
knowing I will not share it with my loved ones.

My heart is not yet singing with joy.

An eight-to-ten-foot tree does not appear in my
living room window this Christmas, so boxes of special
ornaments will remain unopened in the storage room
in hopes of resuming their places on the tree next year.
I miss touching each little piece of Christmases past,
each having its own story, its own significance. I miss
placing them on the tree, each in a just-right location,
while breathing in the aromatic, piney-woods fragrance
of the evergreen, be it a blue spruce, a concolour fir,
or a Scots pine. Last year, I made a video recording of
my decorated tree to music, unveiling the weave of my
Christmas history in song. It included songs from Amy
Grant's, "Home For Christmas," Freddy Cole's, "I Want A

Smile For Christmas," "Baroque Christmas," with pieces by Bach, Handel, and others. While this year I will not have a beautiful live Christmas tree to decorate and trim with ages-old tinsel, one or two strands at a time, and garlands of freshly popped hand-strung popcorn, I am feeling at home and at peace with the holiday decorations that surround me.

The ceramic Christmas tree, my mom's, the one she made in a pottery class in Pennsylvania some 40 years ago, is all lit up. I have turned the key ring at its base and discovered that the tree's music box still plays and to my surprise, I discover that it is playing "The Little Drummer Boy." I had no recollection that this was the tune it played, the very one that was on the 45-rpm record my grandfather, Mom's dad, had given to me when I was a child. I think I still have that 45-rpm in a sleeve of a Pony Tail record carrier that dates back to when I was in the fifth grade.

Mom's cherished Christmas Village is set up and lit. There is the Fish Shoppe, the Wool Shop, the Old Curiosity Shop, the Rare Books Shop, the Green Grocer, the Brownlow house and the Van Tassel house, the Livery, the Bishop's Oast, and the Church. Here comes a horse-drawn carriage, and from the opposite direction comes a stagecoach. A peddler is pushing his cart of hazelnuts and walnuts. Children bundled in winter sweaters, hats, and scarves are putting finishing touches on their snowman. The River Street

Ice House cart is set up for business with horse and driver standing alongside it. The town's one-man band is playing his accordion, his drums strapped onto his back. Is that his sweet puppy wearing a wool sweater and cap, begging for a treat from a passerby? Does he want to play? Is he waiting to hear another tune from his master? A young couple, maybe still in their teens or possibly in their early twenties, is on the ice, one pushing a large swan sled, the other enjoying the glide. On the same side of the park bridge where the town Christmas tree stands, there is a lamppost wrapped in evergreens and bright red berries. The tree is not yet decorated. Perhaps all the town's folk will decorate it on Christmas Eve while singing carols in the town square. No one is walking across the bridge in either direction. A single cardinal, often seen as a sign of good luck or a spiritual message, and a lone bluebird, believed to be a symbol of happiness, harmony, and peace, sit gently on the outer edge of the pool surrounding the sculptured fountain. The hands of the town clock tell the time; it is nearly 8 o'clock. Nobody is seated in the gazebo, nor is anyone on the park bench. Will the carolers be arriving soon?

My eyes move to the cocktail table, to the one nutcracker standing there. It was a gift that Charlie purchased for me during our stay at the Biltmore last year at Christmas. It brings back memories of the first time we saw *The Nutcracker* performed at the New

York State Theatre at Lincoln Center. Our daughter, Maegan, was five years old. Having read parts of E.T.A. Hoffman's *The Nutcracker* to her, we decided to take her to see the magical story performed to music and dance. Driving into New York City the night of the performance, I remembered when I went to Lincoln Center with my Spanish class to see the ballet *Don Quixotec* in 1964. I had not been there since. Maegan's eyes lit up throughout *The Nutcracker* performance; she beamed, awed by the Dance of the Sugar Plum Fairy, the Party Scene, the Land of the Sweets, the wooden Nutcracker doll, Marie's Christmas gift from her Godfather Drosselmeier. She was fascinated by the Matryoshkas (the Russian doll dancers) and Mother Ginger, the giant gingerbread house! As we left the theatre, Maegan asked if she could take ballet lessons.

Also, on my cocktail table are two other Nutcracker characters, Drosselmeier and the Mouse King. I remember buying them though I had not been looking to buy dolls that day. I believe there were two reasons for my purchase. One was the obvious, my fondness for *The Nutcracker*. The expressions on those dolls' faces had me imagining the characters live on stage once again. Secondly, I saw that they were part of a collection by Annalee, and my mom had loved Annalee dolls.

I am drawn to the simple wooden figures of my Nativity set. As a child I remember putting together a number of paper-doll Nativity scenes. Then came the mini-sized molded plastic Nativity scenes. While vacationing in Mexico in the 90s, I found a clay statue of Mary and one of Joseph that I liked and purchased, but it wasn't until the year 2000 that I got this beautiful Nativity complete with Mary holding the baby, Jesus, and Joseph standing by her side in the stable, the three wise men, the shepherds, the sheep and goat, the donkey and the camel, all beneath the North Star.

My memories give my heart joy.

I will not be in church this Christmas Eve, but rather, I will be in my car at a previously recorded drive-in service that will be shown on a big screen and broadcast on radio. It will include the story of Christmas presented by the children of the congregation and beautiful choral and instrumental music. And for the first time since March, when the pandemic began, I will receive Communion bread.

Christmas sings in my heart.

Heading Home in a Pandemic

Carolyn Fore

Our group of eight travelers had already been in Australia for a week when we boarded our massive ship in Sydney for a wonderful cruise to New Zealand on March 8, 2020, aware of the impending pandemic but believing it was still distant from us in both time and proximity. We went about our cruise enjoying the spectacular scenery and only mildly listening to the stories of what was taking place at home as the coronavirus started to spread. On March 15, the day we were in Napier, we heard that the U.S. was limiting international travel and both Australia and New Zealand were closing their borders. We began to worry about getting home. As we were leaving the evening show in the main theater, we felt the ship leaning as if making a sharp turn, and we wondered what was happening. Soon afterwards the captain announced he had turned our ship around and we were heading directly back to Sydney. At this time, we were told to be cautious;

"There are no known cases of coronavirus on the ship but keep a distance from other passengers and call the medical team if you feel sick." It took us three days to get back to Sydney, and during that time we felt like we were in a bubble continuing to enjoy our cruise and celebrating St. Patrick's Day while the rest of the world cancelled their events. Yet we were anxious about what was going on everywhere else. During that time, we continued our activities as usual, but were more diligent about handwashing, use of the wipes we brought with us, and limiting our use of the elevators, or lifts as they were called. While I normally try to use the stairs on cruise ships for the exercise, I made a greater effort to avoid crowded elevators, even if it meant waiting until an empty one came along or walking when I was tired. More than once I got off before my floor when the elevator stopped and too many people got on.

Our last night on the ship, March 18, we tried to have fun but couldn't help talking about our concerns for how we would get home. Our flight from Sydney to Los Angeles had been cancelled, we were arriving back in Sydney two days ahead of schedule, and we had managed to book other flights, but there were so many questions: would we be allowed off the ship, would we be allowed on the flights, would these new flights also be cancelled, what else did we not know that we needed to know? We were told that we needed to quarantine for 14 days and that could possibly be after we got home, or in a hotel in Sydney, or even by remaining on the ship. There were more unknowns than knowns at that time.

The morning we left the ship in Sydney, we walked off and went quickly through customs and immigration handing in the papers we had filled out saying where we had been and that we didn't feel sick. We were given handouts outlining symptoms of coronavirus. These instructed us that we should quarantine when we reached our destination adding that as international travelers we should go directly to the airport and leave the country. If we could not do that, we should quarantine at a hotel until we could get a flight home. That was it! We were free to go to the airport. We were shocked that it was so easy. We had ten hours until our flight. We headed straight to the Sydney International Airport, which was not as busy as it had been when we arrived but was still a hub full of anxious passengers waiting for flights out, watching the boards as flights were cancelled. We sighed in relief as we got on our flight to San Francisco late in the afternoon, no questions asked. I was nervous about it until takeoff when I finally felt a sense of calm.

We expected a health check when landing in San Francisco but went through the usual customs with the one form added that we had become accustomed to filling out listing what countries we had traveled to and stating that we didn't have any coronavirus symptoms.

We were on the lookout for the long lines for health checks and quarantines we had heard about on the news but never saw them.

We waited another ten hours in the nearly empty San Francisco airport before getting on our flight to Atlanta. During that time, we each received a phone call or an email from the New South Wales government informing us that coronavirus had been linked to our ship and to contact them. We all agreed it would be best to wait until we got home. I was adamant that I didn't want to chance being held in the San Francisco airport so we should keep a low profile for now. Since we were on a domestic flight from San Francisco to Atlanta, there were no checks when we landed in Atlanta. The airport was practically empty, even more than usual for 6:00 a.m. We waited for our luggage, and I went outside to wait for our ride. One of our daughters and her husband were picking us up, but they didn't want to be near us in case we had been exposed so they stopped at our house and picked up one of our cars and brought it to us. The airport was so empty they easily pulled both cars up to baggage claim and waved to us before leaving in their car after making sure we were able to get our luggage into our car. No hugs, almost no conversation. Not the usual homecoming. After our more than 30-hour trip, which included two overnight flights, we arrived home exhausted, welcomed by food, toilet paper, and antibacterial soap delivered there by our other daughter. We were set to begin our two-week quarantine.

At the time I thought the story ended there. I settled in for two weeks of reflection and gratitude, so happy to have had a great vacation with a successful trip home. Over the next few months, I learned that many people who had been on our ship contracted Covid-19, and a shocking number died from it. We heard about stories of other travelers that did not end as well as ours which made me even more grateful for our safe outcome and sad for our travel companions. The trip was one of my most memorable, accented by an unforgettable trip home, followed by the pandemic year that will always be part of our histories.

Icon

Christy Baker Knight

In the months leading up to this time—this stranger place we're still navigating—I was feeling burnt out as an Environmental Educator. Gasping for fresh air amid blowers, cars, and construction, our tribe of naturalists struggled to engage a slippery audience of restless children. Often, after traffic delays getting to the urban preserve, we were left with only twenty minutes of free exploration outside. What was free time anyway in this over-scheduled era? Everyone needed a great big nap, preferably in a hammock.

It wasn't that children were indifferent to Nature. They are highly aware of the battle to save Earth from pollution. As one child commented after wrapping pine bark guards around his wrists, "I got some armor for Blue Heron." He did not mean the bird. Our nature preserve is named after the majestic creature because it represents the rejuvenation of that species after pesticides almost wiped them out in the nineteen seventies. Blue Heron Nature Preserve is a place worthy of superhero defense.

With its sword-like bill and six-foot wingspan, the bird has been extensively painted and photographed, like the iconography of Jesus. In February 2020 (right before the world changed), just a mile from the preserve a member of this species got trapped in fishing line in our neighborhood pond. Its majestic wing spread out in flight, hovering in a still pose that would never launch. Tangled in invisible thread suspended over the water, the bird suffered and then died. In pouring rain, the body of this tragic beast was salvaged by beautiful leaders of our community and taken to Blue Heron where Georgia Audubon roosts. There, the body was laid to rest.

An autopsy revealed death by strangulation from a deep-sea fishing weight that had been carelessly used in a pond the size of an Olympic swimming pool. The Christ-Figure bird's death mirrored the low point we had reached, the environmental impact sins that required salvation.

The possibility occurs to me that this virus might heal Earth from a toxic species—Homo sapiens. The world is a juicy plant, and we are the aphids sucking the lifeblood from it. Along comes a biological predator, microscopic ladybugs to save the plant's life. The fact that we have basically been killing our own home makes this fantasy hyperreal. Indeed, one of the silver linings of this time is that we are seeing industry pause and with it a clearing of toxic air. A deep hope is born from darkness, like the resurgence of the Great Blue Heron.

Will He rise again? We are still in day one or two of the holy vigil and cannot yet know. The world waits, sometimes surprisingly with humor and kindness, reminding us that all is not lost. We adapt to a place where family matters most, free time exists, and technology connects us to the deeply loved members of our tribe.

We wait.

We pray.

We heal.

Will it be enough inactivity to save our home?

Psalm 91:4

"and under his wings you will find refuge"

About the Authors

BEVERLY BAKER

B everly Baker is a published writer within the disciplines of art criticism and poetry, and a widely exhibited and collected visual artist. These separate, but mutually compatible, paths have converged since her career began in the mid-1960s. After having attended several art schools, including the Atlanta College of Art, and having participated in an undergraduate degree program at NYU, Beverly finally graduated "With Great Distinction" from San Jose State University, California in 1977 with a Fine Arts BA (Creative Writing major). She was invited to join the Holy Innocents' memoir group by her daughter Christy Knight because there is no comparable group at St. Phillip's Cathedral where Beverly and her family have been members for over forty years. Beverly has been especially appreciative of the Holy Innocents' memoir leaders, Sally Parsonson and Carolyn Fore. She says that it has been an extraordinary experience in Christian Fellowship. In gratitude, she has been donating to Holy Innocents' and is looking forward to post-Covid services. Visit Beverly at fieldandstudio.com.

TONY CLARKE

Tony Clarke was born in 1930 in Washington, D.C.; mother, Lucille Fluckey of Washington, D.C.; father, Gordon Clarke of Boston, Massachusetts, who were married in Washington after completing their education during the depression. In 1935 Tony's parents moved to Lakewood, Ohio, a western suburb of Cleveland. For Tony, the years in Lakewood were idyllic. The family moved to Louisville, Kentucky, in 1943 and in 1945 to Columbia, Kentucky, where his father leased a hotel. Tony went off to college at Harvard following high school, and after his sophomore year, while looking for a summer job, he inadvertently joined a local Kentucky National Guard unit, which was called up for service during the Korean War. Three years in Army artillery, including one year in Korea in 1952, was a significant experience. Leaving the Army in 1955, Tony returned to college and then went on to graduate business school for an MBA. After graduation he joined the U.S. Gypsum Company and then Bankers Leasing Company in Boston, Massachusetts. This began his working career in equipment leasing utilizing his financial training. Retirement from GE Capital Fleet Services ended his working career and placed him in the good years of retirement.

Before attending graduate business school in 1955, Tony married Marilyn Madden of Rockland, Massachusetts, and was blessed with their three children, Beth, Anne (now deceased), and Bill. After their divorce Tony was married to Sally Jean Morse until her death in 1994. At Holy Innocents' Episcopal Church Tony met Peggy Sullivan, with whom he celebrated twenty-five years of marriage in 2021. Tony has enjoyed many interests and activities including membership in several organizations. His major passion for travel has taken him to many places in this country and around the world, including national parks, cities, and memorials in the United States; fishing sites and cities in Canada; most of Western Europe, Ireland, England, Korea, Japan, Austria, Hungary, Peru, Egypt, and Israel. Why travel? For Tony it was to see the beautiful places of this world and experience the wonders of civilization and people everywhere. It's been inspiring to him to acknowledge that humans have such a unique capacity for survival, civilization, and compassion. For him it's a wonderful world we live in and something to cherish with grace and humor.

STEFAN FATZINGER

S tefan Fatzinger was made in Germany but born to a German mother and American father in Bethlehem, Pennsylvania. His parents divorced when he was five, and he and his brother went on to live in foster homes and an orphanage and briefly with his father and stepmother before leaving home entirely and embarking on their own when Stefan was fourteen. He ultimately discovered Washington College Academy in East Tennessee where he was able to work his way through high school. He obtained a B.A. degree from the University of Tennessee and a M.A. from the University of Southern California. He began his working career as a banker in Nashville, Tennessee, then moved on to IBM, before becoming a stockbroker. In the 70s, he left the business world to join the intelligence field in West Germany, landing in Kronach, Germany where he worked for six years in one of the six border resident offices located along the East/West German border during the Cold War. Although he left the world of intelligence in 1988, he would remain in Europe for another eight years working for an American firm, first traveling throughout Europe and the Middle East before transferring to Guam and traveling throughout Asia and the Pacific. In total, Stefan lived overseas for twenty-one years before returning to America to work as a small business consultant traveling throughout the United States and Canada. He retired in 2010, and moved to Atlanta, Georgia, where, having become an Episcopalian while living in Guam, he discovered and became a member of Holy Innocents' Episcopal Church. His life experiences have left him with many stories to tell, but it wasn't until 2014 when Carolyn Fore and Sally Parsonson created a memoir-writing class at Holy Innocents' that he found an outlet that allowed him to begin telling those stories.

CAROLYN WHITE FORE

C arolyn White Fore considers herself a true southerner as she was born in Louisiana and has lived most of her life in Georgia and yet she recognizes that spending six years of her childhood in Pittsburgh, Pennsylvania was influential in her development. Having attended Hollins College, the University of North Carolina, and the University of Georgia, she has multiple degrees which led her from her initial interest in chemistry to her love for computers. She has many years of leadership experience in a corporate environment with responsibility for multigenerational teams. During those years she recognized the differences in the leadership styles of leaders from different generational groups. She wrote her doctoral dissertation at Capella University on next-generation leadership, focusing on millennials as leaders. After retiring from her career in financial information services, she began writing, first about millennials and their leadership style in her book *Millennials Taking the Lead*. She now enjoys teaching in the MBA program at

Brenau University and co-leading the memoir writing group at Holy Innocents' Episcopal Church, where she has been a member most of her adult life. When she is not teaching or writing, she spends her time on her favorite activity which is to be with her children and grandchildren. She enjoys seeing new places and has traveled to all fifty of the states in the U.S. plus Canada and Mexico, in addition to her international travel.

CHRISTY BAKER KNIGHT

A lifelong writer, Christy Baker Knight has been crafting and reading her stories aloud to unsuspecting groups of people since the third grade. She is a featured author in the Wattpad Community with two prize-winning e-books: a water-time mystery novel, *Hot Pressed*, and an environmental fantasy novella, *The Grove*. Her latest work of fiction, *On Display, a novel of natural history*, was released in print fall of 2021 thanks in large part to the support of the Holy Innocents' memoir class. Christy has worked as an exhibit designer for a museum of natural history, as an award-winning botanical illustrator and library muralist perched on scaffolding above voracious readers, and as an art and environmental educator at a nature preserve. A member of Holy Innocents' since 2007, she lives with her family in the Piedmont region of Georgia where she persists while running on the river trails and avoiding calls from someone named Spam Risk. Visit Christy at fieldandstudio.com.

JEANNIE LONGLEY

J eannie Longley was born in Rockford, Illinois to Jean and John VanLandingham, the youngest of five girls, and a surprise to her parents. She graduated from Wellesley College and Northwestern University Medical School prior to completing a residency in Obstetrics and Gynecology, also at Northwestern. After practicing for 15 years, Jeannie took a leave of absence from full-time practice, and never looked back. She volunteered at the Good Samaritan Health Center for a decade, and along with her husband Lester, raised two children. A life-long Episcopalian, Jeannie has been active at Holy Innocents' Episcopal Church for nearly thirty years. Jeannie joined the memoir group in 2016, and has loved hearing the stories of her classmates and contributing her own snippets of life experiences. Jeannie's goal in writing is to relate life stories in a way that will bring a smile to the face of the reader. She enjoys reading, cooking, playing bridge, and being outdoors, especially running. During medical school, Jeannie married Lester, and they recently celebrated their 42nd wedding anniversary. They enjoy biking, hiking, and camping together. Jeannie is the proud mother of Cliff and Dori, and mother-in-law to Suzanne and to John. She and Lester welcomed their first grandchild, Daniel, during the height of the pandemic.

SALLY PARSONSON

Sally Parsonson was born in Memphis, Tennessee, and grew up down the Mississippi River in Greenville. She graduated from Millsaps College in Jackson, Mississippi, and completed her graduate studies with a Ph.D. in English at Tulane University in New Orleans, even farther down the river. After teaching for a few years at Millsaps, she moved to Sandy Springs, transferring from St. James' (Jackson, Mississippi) to Holy Innocents' in 1973. Her daughters Lynn and Beth were active in HI activities, especially the Youth Choir and eventually EYC. Sally briefly taught the third-grade Sunday School class, but soon switched to adult classes with various versions of "Faith and Fiction." In the 1980s, now divorced, she left college teaching to spend several years training Georgia Power garage personnel on a computer-based maintenance system. One day at Holy Innocents', she met Peter Parsonson, a Georgia Tech professor in Civil Engineering, and they were married at Holy Innocents' in 1990. About that time, Sally returned to academia at The Art Institute of Atlanta and took on various roles in administration, including becoming Dean of Academic Affairs. Both of her daughters have settled in Iowa where Lynn is a lawyer in Goldfield (population about 600, but she and her husband, a telecommunications executive, have added five children to that number). Beth and her husband have one son. They teach in different fields at Iowa Central Community College in Fort Dodge, the town where both families attend St. Mark's Episcopal Church.

JANET WILSON

J anet Wilson was born in Bronx, New York and grew up in Yorktown Heights in Westchester County, New York. She attended SUNY Geneseo, was an exchange student at La Universidad de Puerto Rico at Rio Piedras, and later completed her BA in Elementary Education (with a concentration in Spanish) at Pace University in Pleasantville, New York and an MA in Elementary Education and Spanish from Fairfield University, Connecticut. After 30 years of teaching for the Putnam Valley Central School District where she also served as Language Arts Coordinator and Staff Developer, Janet taught SAT Prep at Huntington Learning Centers in both New York and Georgia. She has taught ESOL for La Amistad, the Sandy Springs Mission, and CAC. In addition, she has enjoyed being a Reading Buddy at Lake Forest Elementary School for the Sandy Springs Education Force. Since 2015, Janet has attended Holy Innocents' Episcopal Church where she has been a member of the choir, Reading Connections, and Faith and Fiction. Always a teacher of writing, she now devotes time to her own writing in the memoir group at Holy Innocents'. Her writings are reminiscences of childhood and family relationships. Janet attended child burials officiated by the Reverend Cliff Dawkins at Lakeside Cemetery in Palmetto and describes this outreach involvement as both a privilege and a gift. While teaching has been her passion, her love lies in being a mother, grandmother, great-grandmother, and partner-in-life with Charlie. Charlie and Janet reside in Savannah and Sandy Springs with their best friend, Promise, a Lab/Schnauzer mix, an avid swimmer and fetcher who just loves Morgan Falls on the Chattahoochee.

GEORGE THOMAS

George Thomas was a member of the Holy Innocents' memoir group who participated occasionally but chose not to publish any of his work in this book. We, however, very much enjoyed hearing some of his memoirs which included tales of a country boyhood in South Carolina, high school memories, and his accounts of his work early in his law career at the U. S. Patent Office in Washington, D. C.

About the Book

View images from the memoirs and learn about author news and events here:

https://www.fieldandstudio.com/theplacelightgetsin/

Special thanks to Words of Passion for their expert work on the cover and layout, along with their patience in working through the challenges of publishing a book with eight authors.

Made in USA - Kendallville, IN
26978_9780578336701
03.10.2022 1022